Sharpe Cut

The Inside Story of the Creation of a Major Television Series

LINDA BLANDFORD

HarperCollins*Publishers*

HarperCollins*Entertainment*
An Imprint of HarperCollins*Publishers*
77–85 Fulham Palace Road,
Hammersmith, London W6 8JB

www.harpercollins.co.uk

Published by HarperCollins*Entertainment* 2006
1

All photographs by Tony Nutley © Sharpe Challenge Ltd except the following:

pp 5-6 Sharpe book covers © HarperCollinsPublishers.
(Jacket photographs by Tony Nutley © Sharpe Challenge Ltd)

p15 (bottom), 23, 24, 27, 55, 63, 69, 75, 78, 84, 85, 91 (bottom), 106, 107 (top) 132,
135, 151, 152, 153, 154, 165, 166, 168, 183, 185, 190, 200, 203, © Linda Blandford

A catalogue record for this book
is available from the British Library

ISBN-13: 978 0 00 723214 7
ISBN-10: 0 00 723214 4

Set in Minion

Printed and bound in Great Britain by
Butler and Tanner

For Anthony Smith,
the best of godfathers

Contents

The Trailer

In November, winter sets into Rajasthan, days shorten and I'm walking through a night of total and eerie blackness. I sense rather than see the hills rolling far off into the burning Rajasthan desert sands. Out there are tigers, leopards, villages where fire is the only light, a proud warrior race of Rajputs descended from the gods, relics of kingdoms and Croesus wealth astride destitution, layer upon layer of invasion and conquest. Jaighar Fort stands on the top of a mountain overlooking a lake where elephants bathe during the day and tourist buses fill the air with choking pollution and noise. But now there is only dark silence and a clammy awareness of dead men's bones in this monument to war and bloodshed.

Such is the thickness of the fort walls that rounding the corner into the light and commotion comes almost as an explosion in itself. There's the sickening stench and eye-streaming smoke of burning cow dung in steel platters. It's the smell of celluloid bloodshed and warfare which hangs over most weeks of *Sharpe's Challenge*. On the top of one wall, rockets shower into the night air from a high battlement wall, fired by Pindari soldiers in thin, cotton dress. The Indians were the first to use rockets in battle: hence the irony that getting them to work here has been the bane of *Sharpe's Challenge*. That they go off at all is greeted, in what passes for celebration, with dull grunts. Time to move on: tiny women, fleshless men and a few burly technicians dismantle the heavy tons of camera equipment.

At the end of a long tunnel nearby, the waiting crew huddle around tea

OPPOSITE: *Sean and Hermit,*
his spirited polo pony

and coffee urns set out on a trestle table in an ancient arch. They drink quickly – the cold bites. I know this cold from the Empty Quarter of Saudi: it's the dry, desert bitterness that no number of puffy jackets and woolly hats can keep out. Some try, and this explains the presence of what seems to be a flock of fat scarecrows scattered around the courtyard. Others brazen it out in thin fleeces and even shorts. Macho man's badge of honour.

In the centre of the courtyard is a skinny blonde actor in a dusty, frayed flimsy uniform surveying a hefty bullock cart stuffed with sandbags and rockets. He's covered in blood and the neck of his shirt is pulled open. He's been waiting for hours and must be frozen to the bone. He turns to share a joke with his companion, a man with the build of a stone monument. That Sean Bean can smile still comes as a surprise: it's two weeks into filming and 'cold' is the word most of the crew use of him.

Suddenly, it's all movement. Sean and Daragh O'Malley as his faithful Harper pick up the bullock cart handles and run with it turning the corner into the tunnel. Run? It's taken four men to haul it slowly into place, and more to move it back afterwards. And this is just a rehearsal. There are three takes. Each time, Sean and Daragh have to pick up the cart, build up momentum before getting into shot, and then run hell-for-leather into the tunnel. This in itself is some feat: the ground is uneven, the light thrown

Nigel back behind camera A, Sean takes stock

up by the burning torches is not only dim but sets off the dust. The run takes 12 seconds. And everything I need to know about the next five weeks' shooting is right there.

There are, maybe, 50 people standing around watching this scene. All of them are working on the film. Most of them are men. And not one of them stirs to give the cart a push to get it going. Finally, the young second assistant director, who has strolled in to see how it's all going, shoves his shoulder into the back of the cart for the last take.

Let's deal first with Sean: he stays up late, doesn't have a trainer on set – actually he doesn't have a trainer period – hasn't once worked out, will never be sighted in the fancy hotel gym and yet, compared to the large, hulky Daragh, he's the one who picks up the speed. He has fast hands, fast feet and extraordinary balance on the rocky cobbles.

Why am I surprised? If he had the choice, he'd probably swap all his success for the chance to play a lesser league football. This is the actor who once made a small, overlooked film, *When Saturday Comes*, for the opportunity to run onto a football pitch with Sheffield United. And because he's a loner, a fearless, rugged terrier of a man, he'd drop with fatigue before he'd ask for help. And because he's the star, the crew wouldn't have the guts to suggest he could do with it. Besides, it's all about testing and challenging, about seeing whether or not the bugger can pull it off. Welcome to the world of Richard Sharpe and 'boys' stuff'.

A word of explanation: in the film, the Fort is held by a 'rebel' Maharajah holding out against the invading British. The tunnel leads to a mine which is meant to explode as the attacking troops storm into a breach, thereby decimating the Brits. Naturally, only our two heroes can save the day. Or, rather, the night. The setting off of the explosion is filmed over four nights in minute segments.

The night shoots start at 6.00 in the evening and go on until 5.00 in the morning. Yes, I know that nurses, lorry drivers and others all do nights and change it around regularly with day work. They don't, on the other hand, do it after waiting around in this mean cold, nor in a narrow tunnel filled with smoke, in the dark, waiting for deafening and potentially dangerous explosions to be set off by special effects. Well, not dangerous because they're controlled by men who blow up buildings and airplanes without a blink but it certainly requires a major degree of trust.

There are eight steel mortars at the end of this tunnel each filled with bleached dust and rubble, kilos of black explosive powder and two 8oz electrical charges. This is India, a country on high security alert. It's forbidden to buy more than one 10kg bag of black powder at a time, and even when you do, you're not sure what you've actually got. Sometimes, it's black, sometimes it's grey and sometimes black with grey, which means there's flash powder mixed into it. Black powder deflagrates or burns, flash powder explodes. And even when it's black, the powder won't be predictable. No two bags explode the same way nor are the electrical charges any more reliable than the powder. It's all the difference between control and SFX anarchy. This is special effects as code-breaking. And by this time, everyone knows it. There are no secrets on a film set.

So Tony Auger, the special effects' supervisor, wanders over to Sean and Daragh who are tucked into a nook halfway down the tunnel and explains in his matter of fact way, what is to happen. One can only admire his air of cool confidence. There won't in fact be one explosion because it could set off a shock wave strong enough to blow open the wall. Not good for the actors or for the stuntmen hovering at the other end of the tunnel, not to mention the cameraman set up not far behind Sean, nor Tony himself who will be right there. The eight cauldrons will fire one after the other in a ripple effect to set off a lot of little shock waves and as long as Sean and Daragh tuck their heads down and close their eyes, they'll be fine. It'll look like one big explosion to the naked eye. No complaints from Sean, no questions; he listens, nods and waits. He just stands there. And everyone else carries on as normal – swigging bottles of water, talking about shopping, shivering in the freezing night, rocking slightly with tiredness.

And then the tunnel explodes. It's a total white out. Dust billows out of the tunnel. Terrifying. Sean emerges, brushes down his jacket, reaches for a cigarette and a cup of tea, and rummages through his brown leather bag. No one goes up to him. No one says a word. It's as if nothing happened.

Sharpe
BERNARD CORNWELL
SHARPE'S TIGER

Sharpe
BERNARD CORNWELL

SHARPE'S FORTRESS

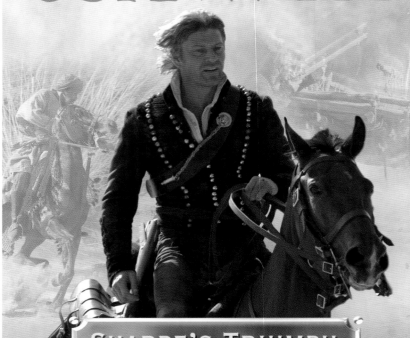

Sharpe

BERNARD
CORNWELL

SHARPE'S TRIUMPH

The Backstory

Some say it was on the beach at Nikolaevka, others that it was in a car park outside Simferopol. It's branded in producer Muir Sutherland's memory that it was in a school car park adjacent to the beach at Nikolaevka, and he should know. It doesn't much matter now where it happened. What does matter is that it set off the most expensive insurance claim – for £2m – in the history of British television. On 16 August, 1992, two days into the shooting of the first *Sharpe* film in Ukraine, Paul McGann, its eponymous star, fell over during a friendly game of football. Nothing too dramatic; at first, he seemed to have twisted his ankle. No such luck. He'd torn the anterior cruciate ligament in his knee. Even with aggressive sports medicine, it could have taken him six months to a year to be strong enough for scrambling up hills, leaping onto horses or storming Napoleon's battlements.

It's even harder, all these years later, to pinpoint anyone who was crazy about casting McGann in the first place. As *Sharpe*'s casting director, the wise and grizzled John Hubbard, puts it: 'Success has many fathers; failure is an orphan.' Perhaps it's that other adage about a camel being a racehorse designed by committee – when feelings run high, the least offensive actor gets the part. Anyway, out went the talented but injured McGann, out too went the tetchy director and leading lady. And on 5 October, one week after the filming was cancelled and the whole unit flown home from Ukraine, they piled back onto an Aeroflot flight with a new Richard Sharpe – Sean Bean.

When Rufus Sewell and the two McGann brothers, Paul and Mark, were tested for the part, Sean didn't even get a call. The writer's daughter, it's said, didn't like him. 'Sean was the obvious choice from the start,' Hubbard now says. 'He had heroism, he was a loner, a man's man, gentle with women. And when the insurance company wouldn't wait any longer, I said to Malcolm Craddock: "Let's not muck about – let's cast Sean Bean"' Received wisdom has it that Bean, chippy, driven, testy before slights and fresh from matching Harrison Ford scene for scene in *Patriot Games*, demanded to be paid twice whatever McGann's salary had been.

'I don't remember that,' Sean says, 'but I did want to know things were right. I felt pretty comfortable with the character but it was new territory and they weren't ready for what Russia was going to hit them with. They were all sick and came back the first time looking like skeletons. I thought: "Fuck me, what am I getting into?"'

The salary story is told by veterans of the early *Sharpe* films which were shot in a shaky, newly-independent Ukraine, by the veterans of hours spent hanging out in a freezing army tent when Sean was just one of the blokes, before success spawned his trailer. Apocryphal story, maybe, but a reminder that in the end, for all the talk about 'art' and 'loving the part' – being appreciated is always about money. Actually, in film almost every-thing's about money, and whatever isn't, is about luck. Today, Paul McGann is a highly respected actor; Sean Bean is an international star.

Muir Sutherland of Celtic Films and Malcolm Craddock of Picture Palace produced 14 wildly popular *Sharpe* films over five years. They are an odd couple. Muir is garrulous, generous, good company, a bull of a man with a lurking hint of aggression. Mention Malcolm Craddock's name in the business and you'll get one answer: 'He's a good man'. This is not to mistake caring and gentleness for weakness – instinct tells me that he ran from those qualities quite successfully for long, long years and has come to them slowly. Take a look at any edition of *Broadcast* magazine peopled by the young, and in their very survival, Sutherland and Craddock have about them a hint of *The Muppets*' Statler and Waldorf, the toffs who barrack from the balcony, embodying the revenge of age.

Together they were responsible for one of ITV's biggest popular successes, but also, one year later, *A Life for a Life*, the heart-rending true story of Stefan Kiszko, a mentally challenged man wrongly convicted of murder, destroyed by 15 years in prison. That they had to fight for years to make the programme is no surprise: an audience of 8 million was their tribute. So, nothing about them is altogether as it appears. They are at an age where they are the sum of their experiences – and neither of them has always had an easy ride.

Having said that, in the last champagne-Charlie years of British television – the 70s and 80s – Muir Sutherland flew around the world for about a third of the year, and argued over exactly which first-class seat he was prepared to sit in. He was a captain of Thames Television in the days when commercial TV was, in the famous words of Lord Thomson, owner of Scottish Television, 'a licence to print money'. He was a spectacular success as head of international sales ('£10 million or something like that and a Queen's Award for exports'), and finally Thames' Head of Programmes. It was the Bel Air in Los Angeles, the Carlton at Cannes ('a suite with a balcony'), a couple of hundred Christmas cards coming and going, 'an almost unlimited expense account', the Ivy and the driver in the company Jaguar waiting outside.

Son of an oil man, whose wife died when Muir was 3, the boy was brought up by a widowed aunt. A graduate of a Scottish public school and PPE (philosophy, politics and economics) at Oxford, Muir Sutherland found himself in the rough-and-tumble of rugby and field hockey, and later in the cut-throat milieu of commercial television. He must have been a fearsome and pugnacious fighter – he would have had needed to be in order to swallow his unexpected departure, when in his 50s, from Thames, and the six-year battle which ensued to make the first Sharpe films as an independent producer. He's 72 years old now, ebullient, sharp and a showman, but no one would describe him as soul-searching – not even, after 35 years, his devoted Spanish wife, Mercedes.

Producers come in all sizes and varieties. They are there at the beginning; they are there at the end. Not the honorary producers, the myriad of 'producer' credits for those who come up with vital money after the years of fund-raising, or those who make one phone call to those who will provide funding, or the star's agent who manages not to obstruct the deal – such producers and executive producers stand in relation to the real thing much as Princess Michael of Kent does to royalty. No, producers actually make the film happen and almost always against impossible odds. The survivor's endurance and optimism would have to be requirements for the job and Muir and Malcolm have both.

Well, perhaps Malcolm Craddock doesn't have optimism so much as hope. He'll go on trying no matter what. When something – or more often someone – pains him, his face shrinks and the small cathedral chorister from St Albans is written there. The penumbra of good intention surrounds him. His father was a cautious-natured clerk with the Prudential, an ex-POW who must have learned the hard way to value safety. When the son stood on the stairs, stomach churning as he opened the letter telling him he had won an open scholarship to Cambridge, he remembers to this day his dour father's reaction: 'You're not going.' Reaching beyond oneself wasn't safe half a century ago in lower-middle-class Harpenden.

Maybe that struggle explains the later flamboyant career directing commercials, making tons of money, the glossy Soho offices, a staff of 40, drinking as a way of life. Maybe he was marked indelibly by his battle against osteomyelitis and septicaemia since 1969, by not being able to work for three years and consequently losing his house. Much of his struggle now is with his acceptance of faith, his coming to terms with the death of his daughter, Emily, in the Amazon two years ago, and trying to make 'good' pictures, ones with 'value', all the while jostling the reality of making *Sharpe* dazzle on a locked budget. It says much about him that his hero isn't that Hollywood superstar, Steven Spielberg, but Saul Zaentz, the very singular producer of such distinguished Oscar-winning films as *One Flew over the Cuckoo's Nest*, *Amadeus* and *The English Patient*.

In 1989, when Muir phoned and asked him to come on board for *Sharpe*, Malcolm was in the Caribbean producing the 4-part TV series, *The Orchid House*. It speaks well of Muir that he offered Craddock a 50:50 partnership, given the work and money Sutherland had already invested in the project. But Malcolm Craddock was not only a shrewd producer but also a friend. 'We had dinner in each other's houses,' as Muir puts it, to emphasize the reality of this friendship.

Entering the private realm is a major watershed in media relationships in Britain, where the private/public division is still strong. Why else are there all those private clubs and restaurants mobbed by London telly types who are nominally 'friends' but not when it comes to a tight, competitive corner? It is revealing, for instance, that even now, 13 years later, neither Malcolm nor Muir have been invited to dinner at home with Sean. On the other hand, they haven't invited him over either. Anyway, these two producers were friends. And they needed to be. Many a trial lay ahead in filming *Sharpe*: famine, drought, actors' strikes, the Mafia, giardia lamblia and cholera to mention but a few.

At this point, however, the commercial company Central Television had merely promised Muir that they would back the *Sharpe* films. All he had to do was prise the film option away from the BBC which had been sitting on it for years. In the euphoria of perestroika, when the Evil Empire had metamorphosed into the friendly bear, no one was thought to be interested in tales of the British army, rampant and triumphant. The BBC, of course, is known as an organization where a dozen people can say 'no', but only one can say 'yes' – and would rather not in case it's a mistake. (Not for nothing was Alan Yentob's affectionate nickname as the BBC's Head of Drama 'Forever Amber'.) *Sharpe* tumbled meekly into Muir's determined hands – or more correctly, Central's who then owned the rights and made almost all the money when it finally became a wild success. Or more correctly still, Andy Allen, Central's director of programmes, who had been Head of News at Thames, was the one who pointed his old boss towards the languishing *Sharpe*. Television is about 'relationships', for which, even now, read boozy lunches. Back then, Central was prepared to put £420,000 into the development and pre-production. Later they agreed to commit to £620,000 per hour for three two-hour films to go out in one season. Muir and Malcolm together worked out a budget which, at its tightest, came out at something like £700,000 a film. Hopeless, or so it would have seemed to most anyone else.

Undaunted, they went off to investigate shooting in Spain, Slovenia and

Montenegro. All were too expensive. The Soviet Union was Central's novel idea: this was still perestroika time and Central had recently formed a joint documentary venture with the Russians. The East-West Creative Association was going to provide it all, a job-lot – and cut-price: crew, costumes, make-up, catering, extras, hotels and loads of vodka.

By the time the rickety Aeroflot plane had landed in the Crimea, Gorbachev had fallen and Ukraine was in a state of mayhem, the political order suspended, with nuclear submarines laid up like monsters in the Black Sea. There's a Chinese curse: 'May you live in interesting times'. These times were interesting. Before they left, word went out to actors and crew to bring their own toilet rolls, bath plugs, and a warning that food wasn't great (a euphemism for 'most Ukrainians are starving').

Listen now to Muir and you'll hear wonderful stories about crew camaraderie in Simferopol, the beauty of Yalta, sauntering through the airport with $30,000 cash stuffed into his pocket, the enthusiasm of the military recruits as they re-enacted the Napoleonic wars, the feats of the amazing Russian fixer, Igor Nosov – grandson of one of the Czar's generals, son of a Soviet general, close friend of an all-important local Crimean general. 'Igor gave a considerable bung to the Ukrainian general and we got all the soldiers we wanted. Igor could fix anything.' Memory takes Malcolm differently: filming in the Crimea taught him that life can always be worse, and probably will be. It put wire through his spine. He doesn't cave in because he learned under fire that whatever it takes, this is what he loves.

Muir isn't entirely wrong in remembering the Crimea with such affection. With nothing to do, nowhere much to go and all the actors and crew staying in the same KGB sanatorium, swatting the same cockroaches and partying in the one bar, nearly everyone agrees that there was an amazing spirit. The actor Jason Salkey, aka Rifleman Harris, has made a series of video diaries of those early years which he sells on the internet: chronicled for ever is the time he cleaned up £600 throwing wire coat hangers blindfolded onto a clothes rail. This game, as Sean remembers it, took up hours and hours of practising while they shivered in their tent. It's that one tiny puffer heater in the corner, nearly blowing itself to bits, which brings it all home.

'I suppose in a sense those times in the tent were the best times,' Sean says ruefully. 'It was hard, fucking hard but we stuck together.' So why the 'star trailer' thing in the third season? 'In the end I got fed up with living in a tent and I just felt why not, why not a fucking trailer? Sometimes you need solitude. But did you see it? It was an old minibus with a bed stuck in the back.' Then one of those rare and irresistible Bean grins: 'Not that I spent much time in it – I thought "it's fucking boring in here."'

Much of that close spirit comes through in those first early films: the freezing wind gusting over Sean Bean and his small group of 'chosen men' from the 95th Rifles, the skeltering runs through cold, fast-flowing rivers, Sean's embarrassment at being dressed as a monk to pick a church lock, the throat-catching deaths and burials. If this was boys' stuff, it was action with wonderful tales, high energy and a roll-call of distinguished British character actors.

Unfortunately, two of them – Brian Cox and David Troughton – refused to go back to the Crimean hardship when the series was signed for a second year. But watching the 14 early *Sharpe* films is to spot future British stars in the making. Sean himself, of course, who tapped into his intense, Northern bloody-mindedness and created a Sharpe indivisible from the actor. But also watch for Daniel Craig, the new Bond, at the time slightly plump and meanly sardonic as Lt Berry in the second film, *Sharpe's Eagle*. Liz Hurley was ravishing in *Sharpe's Enemy*, an episode which went out the same summer she walked the red carpet in 'that' Versace dress at the premiere of *Four Weddings and a Funeral*. Every producer's dream: you hire a starlet and transmit a star. This is not to overlook the young Paul Bettany, concealing the intelligence and sensitivity of his later role to Russell Crowe's *Master and Commander*, and shining as the foppish and murderously incompetent Prince William of Orange, in the magnificent and last film, *Sharpe's Waterloo*.

Waterloo, in 1997, was the finale. 'There's no reason why it stopped, although Sean certainly didn't want to do any more,' remembers Malcolm Craddock. 'I wanted to do other work and Sharpe was hanging on like a favourite uncle who overstays his welcome.' The Napoleonic Wars were over, Sean was about to get his first international lead as Vronsky in a glamorous production of *Anna Karenina*, Malcolm and Muir were full of hope about other projects on the go, and Carlton Television, which had folded Central into itself, had made its money back over and again.

So how much did the producers make from it in the end – peak-time transmissions with 10 and 12 million viewers, repeats, half a million boxed DVD sets sold and countless videos before those? Did it make them rich? Forget even asking – no one talks about money earned – but probably nowhere near what you'd guess. 'Modest, not breathtaking', is all Malcolm will offer. Sean, at his most open, curls up like a hedgehog at the question. Maybe they were just tired. Whatever the reasons, *Sharpe* seemed to be over for everyone except the novels' original author, Bernard Cornwell, who carried on writing books as if nothing had happened on the small screen. His *Sharpe* book sales had doubled with the films, although he'd hit the bestseller lists before them.

There was one wrinkle: Muir and Malcolm's shrewd lawyer had written a clause into the original deal, probably overlooked at the time. After five years without a *Sharpe* film being made by the commercial company, the underlying rights to the celluloid *Sharpe* would revert to the two producers. *Sharpe's Challenge*, which belongs to Sutherland and Craddock, is the result. Statler and Waldorf have triumphed. Champagne, then, to Frank Bloom who first met Muir in 1969 when he did a house conveyancing for him, the lawyer to whom the producer had stuck ever since through thick times and thin. The film business, as I was to remember again and again, is *all* about relationships.

Sean: it's all in the eyes

Malcolm and Muir: the triumph of age and experience

TAKE 1

Title Sequence – The Read-Through

It is the middle of October and an unexpectedly warm autumn day in London. Two days earlier, the director of *Sharpe's Challenge*, Tom Clegg, was in India clambering up and down hills and across desert valleys looking for possible locations. It was his fourth visit. Filming starts in three weeks time in Jaipur; there are forts to build, ambushes to place, battles to plan. Nevertheless, he has flown back to London for today's read-through at the Shaftesbury Avenue Baptist Church, and tomorrow he'll be back on the plane to Delhi.

Tom Clegg is in his 70s and fitter-looking than the knot of men pulling on a final cigarette outside the church. Its doors stand open under a one-word sign: POVERTY. Appropriate, as it turns out. At first I'm not sure whether the men filing reluctantly inside are anything to do with the film. For all I can tell, they might as well be on their way to an AA meeting or a soup kitchen as the massed talent behind *Sharpe's Challenge* making for the first (and only) script read-through.

It's not a distinguished looking crowd waiting their turn for the small lift to the fourth floor: worn jeans, scuffed trainers, scruffy T-shirts. The look is intentional: wearing their oldest clothes is a demonstration if not of confidence, at least of the appearance of confidence. It's an announcement: 'I have the job now.'; or even 'A job. *At last.*' For sure they didn't dress like this for the meeting with the producer or the audition with the casting director.

There's more to it, though. The read-through is an industry ritual. It has a talismanic function, like walking the fields to bless the crops before the seeds are sown. Dressing down is a demonstration that this ritual is out of time, not part of the process. No need to don the Sunday best, so to speak. It's the one moment of blanket equality, of sitting together around one table – literally, but also symbolically. All too soon, the divisions will be apparent – them the stars, us the jobbing also-rans; them the actors, us the crew; them in production, us who take what we're given. And besides that, it is the one time that all the actors are together. Filming is scheduled so that they can be flown out to India to shoot all their scenes in as few days as possible, and then bundled off home. So for this one special morning, there is the bonhomie of professionals in a tough industry, sharing the glorious feeling that, for a few short weeks, regular money will be going into the bank.

If Hollywood is about 'schmoozing', British television, always under threat of yet more redundancies, even bigger cuts, is big on 'bonding'. Insecurity and low pay make for emotional intensity. Nothing about the future can be taken for granted. Every day, every pitch, every performance starts out as zero-sum. For all the nonchalant posing that will go on this morning, nerves are never far from the surface. It comes out in moments of laughter, laughter that is almost always out of proportion to the joke. It comes out in the way that those who've met before, leap upon their acquaintance. As it happens, not all the actors are here. Some have only just been signed, while somewhere in the casting director's office is a collection of tapes still awaiting the producer and director's last-minute decision. Actors in India, actors in France, actors out on the road elsewhere. Seven years in the planning: months in the financing and the deal only done for sure a few weeks ago. Not surprisingly, in television, almost everything happens at the last moment, and sometimes not even then. Many's the crew member who's got on a plane only to find the project has collapsed by the time he arrives.

This is how the read-through works. By the door is a table laden with hot drinks, sticky buns and some fruit. Food in this situation is not about energy. It's about 'being family', particularly important when budgets are tight and contract offers were low. Apart from the copiously repeated thanks for turning up, which will soon be offered (as if any actor who could, wouldn't), comfort food is the earliest and cheapest way of signalling appreciation, so generosity matters, £150 worth of it. An enormous pile of Danish will be devoured, to be superseded by trays laden with sandwiches. Actors are notorious scroungers. It's why, if and when they make it big, present-giving becomes such a self-conscious and ostentatious habit – compensation for years of hardship and struggle. Meanwhile, the temptation of anything free never goes away; the memory of hard times is too ingrained. Just think of the scrabble for freebie bags at awards ceremonies.

The director, Tom Clegg, wanders down to the far end of the long, rectangular table, and is quickly flanked by various producers, indeterminate production staff, and assorted administrators. Once they've seen where he is positioning himself, the actors shuffle like schoolboys to sit as far away from the headmaster's gaze as possible. In the distance, a special place is held by the door at the entrance to the drab hall. Sean Bean hovers there on his mobile. Of course, he's the only person to use his mobile in the hall. Droit de seigneur. But nor is it a coincidence that his back is right by the exit. There's a haunted, animal-look to him – eyes upon him or not, he's the totem, the star, the object of worship. After all, he's the money.

Bernard Cornwell, the absent author of the *Sharpe* novels, might have served the films' producers better had he made Wellington's horse the hero of the series rather than Sharpe, the sergeant who saved his life. Once an actor makes a part his own, he becomes the one given in a production: only he can hold it to ransom. John Thaw *was* Inspector Morse, as Leo McKern not his creator, John Mortimer, owned Rumpole, and, for that matter, imagine *Prime Suspect* without Helen Mirren. The actor becomes the monopolist of his or her own image. Hence Mirren became the highest paid star in British television when she signed for *Prime Suspect 5*. My guess at this point is that Sean Bean wouldn't walk out of his front door for a big movie part for less than half a million pounds, and that may be insulting him. Open season, then, on how much of the £4 million *Sharpe* budget is going to its star, or, rather, how little his agent would settle for.

That said, here is everything Sean Bean doesn't have: minders, groupies, a line in sincere and unconvincing greetings, small talk, airs and graces. He looks ravaged. His jeans are full of designer holes, his sweatshirt a dull camouflage. His is the antithesis of the Tom Cruise mould of stardom which goes: 'Here I am being electric, flashing my smile hither and yon.' Bean's is no less self-conscious for all that. The more he shrinks into himself, hangs his head low over the scripts, the more he draws the energy of the room towards him. Charisma is inexplicable. To Hollywood, he may still be a highly-paid character actor; in this grey, badly-lit room, stardom shines on his unkempt, blonded hair.

In short order, the table settles to work. The director, Tom Clegg, has the dependable look of a sturdy North Country vet who's lived through more than his share of foot-and-mouth. Clegg's voice is quiet, reasonable; he can afford to be and, anyway, it's his style. He settled long ago into his skin. He's big on twinkles and charm; he's a Director – they go with the job. At this stage, anyway. And, besides, there are others to do the barking for him. Pro forma, the director goes round the table asking people to introduce themselves and their role. This is the first inkling of the division of sheep and goats, crew and actors.

In the years when I wandered in and out of the film world, it was always to profile and interview actors. Dancing around those precarious egos and tempers, there was no time to notice the other men – and yes, mostly men – milling around a set. The crew were anonymous to me back then. This morning, I pick up where confidence lies: not with the actors, but with the men and women with hooded eyes, taking notes, leaning back comfortably in their chairs or forward on the tables, those with skills and titles before their names. Director of Photography, Make-Up Designer, Costume Designer. It's the actors' body language that speaks of uncertainty and the need to please. Interesting to see who among them listens hard to others, who is clearly waiting for his/her turn and makes the announcement with a dash too much eager panache. Nice touch, Bean says: 'Sean Bean – Sharpe', in an expressionless voice.

The reading begins. Only someone close to the man on a far corner might notice the way his lips move through almost every line, albeit hidden behind a bush of whiskers and shoulder-length hair. This isn't Robbie Coltrane in *Harry Potter*; it's Russell Lewis, the script writer. This is when the words pass out of his possession, and, even now, he doesn't know what will or won't work.

It isn't cool to give a performance at the first read through. Actors who are confident enough, play under the lines. 'This is no big deal for me' is the message they send out. Actors who are arrogant have been known to read deliberately quietly so that everyone has to strain to hear them. Sometimes, though, it's strategic: don't give it away too soon. The Reading Recast strikes fear deep into the actor's underemployed psyche. The large, expansive performances come from veterans of the old *Sharpe* films, brought back by 'popular' demand: Peter-Hugo Daly (Sgt Shadrach Bickerstaff) second villain-in-chief, goes way over the top. It's misjudged and smacks either of nerves or of neediness. Not a face flickers at the headmaster's end of the table. The crew, though, take note. Eyelines cross.

Michael Cochrane (General Sir Henry Simmerson – snob and bully) plays equally broad. Evidently, he can get away with it: he and Bean go way back to the first season of *Sharpe*. When Bean didn't trust the Aeroflot plane bringing the unit back from the Crimea to Moscow, Cochrane went with him across Russia by train. Being comfortable with the big star of the show, as well as being naturally good-humoured, is its own permission. Somehow Cochrane picks up the scent and his outrageous reading gives everyone a much-needed chance to laugh, to let go, to let off steam. How does he know? Perhaps, he doesn't: when they're team players good actors read atmosphere and response on automatic pilot.

And what of Bean? Here is the consummate voice-over talent at work. The voice of Britain's Morrison supermarket chain who can give significance to a dressed leg of lamb, the soulful appeal of Imperial Cancer (UK), of the O$_2$ mobile phone network, of National Geographic narrations – dark, coloured, every line delivered with faultless individuality, and not a second of display. If this is one of the camera's natural peacocks, here it neither struts nor fans its tail. And yet his lines draw in the room, each one met by the silence in which the proverbial pin is heard to drop. This isn't obeisance to the money. It's called talent. It's a long time since Bean has carried a show as a romantic lead. The question everyone must be asking is this: now in his middle age, can he do it again?

The answer will lie in the desert state of Rajasthan, 7,000 miles away, when filming starts on location next month. But Sean likes the Four Seasons Hotel in Los Angeles, or the comfort of his local pub in London. Word already has it that Sean Bean isn't looking forward to India. Neither, at this point, am I.

Early tomorrow I fly out to Delhi and the morning after on to Jaipur for a rough, two-day technical recce with 20 or so members of the production team. We'll be walking for hours under the blazing October sun. I don't have a hotel room and this is the height of the tourist season. The *Sharpe's Challenge* production office in Jaipur has sent word that they're too busy booking rooms for 31 UK crew, 66 Indian crew, 8 Russian stuntmen and 86 construction workers from Mumbai so, sorry, you'll have to sort it yourself. But this morning has made one message clear: in television, don't ever let the blokes smell weakness.

Tom Clegg directs another massacre

Making a plan to blow the breach

The Director Goes On A Recce

By the time I arrive in India, someone at the Hilton office in Singapore has put me in touch with the general manager of the Trident-Hilton in Jaipur who takes me in for now, at least. Opposite the hotel, there is a lake in the middle of which appears to float a deserted, fairytale pink palace. The sight of water is the most precious of gifts in this dry northern state and symbolizes the Trident-Hilton's luxurious hush for the 21st-century tourist. It stands outside a city which hovers somewhere between the 9th and 18th centuries and over which hangs the smoggy haze of Los Angeles. The dissonances of the next two months already strike into the soul.

For this incomparable haven, the full rate is £65 a night. I mention this because by paying my own way through India, I buy independence which makes the producers' grant of total freedom to roam both risky and extraordinary. I may have been teaching for years but once a journalist, always a journalist. This is why what happens on the recce today and tomorrow neither surprises nor offends me.

At first, at breakfast, all is well. Since no one introduces me (or anyone else, for that matter), the assumption is made that I'm the producer's wife. As soon as word spreads to the contrary, which in a film crew takes no time, I am ignored by those who don't want to appear to curry favour and

OPPOSITE: *Jaigarh Fort*

am treated with unconvincing charm by some who do. This, I say to myself, remembering the way Sean Bean was treated at the read-through, is how it must feel to be an actor. I mean to hold on to the thought, but probably won't.

Thirty-six hours after leaving the Shaftesbury Avenue Baptist Church, the *Hindustan-Times* hangs in a neat linen bag outside each bedroom door bringing news on page 1 of Catherine Zeta Jones' family camping trip in her landscaped California garden and, buried elsewhere, of ethnic violence around India, of nuclear deals with the USA, of burgeoning warmth with China, and edgy exchanges with next-door Pakistan. There's reality for you.

The Trident-Hilton is soft and rich. The reality of Jaipur is captured over the road from the hotel, on a scrap of waste ground, in a village of cardboard and plastic tents where children play barefoot among feral dogs, foraging boars, wandering cows and filthy water supplies. And if there's a historical affront in 300 outsiders from London, Paris, Moscow, Mumbai, Goa and New Delhi flying, trucking and driving in to the desert foothills of Rajasthan to recreate the British Raj of 200 years past, none of the silky smooth staff in the Trident-Hilton would be insensitive enough to suggest as much.

By 7 o'clock, director Tom Clegg is downstairs at the Trident-Hilton, bobbing with excitement, eagerly awaiting the 20 or so members of the *Sharpe's Challenge* team to set off on the technical recce. I have no idea yet who anybody is, nor does anyone try to enlighten me. All I know is that first we're off to scour Jaigarh Fort, the hills and forest around it, and then to the desert where a fort and village are to be built in an empty valley at Samode. It'll be a long, hard slog. No quarter asked nor given for the exhausting trip to Jaipur from London via a scrabbling madness at either Delhi or Mumbai airport. Everyone turns up on time. 'Alcoholism, drug abuse, divorces left, right and centre,' says one lugubrious crew member, 'but lateness – never.'

A director can be many things. In the movie world, he can be auteur, martinet, megalomaniac, cocaine addict or plain journeyman who can brown-nose stars from their trailers near enough on time. In Hollywood a picture can be a gigantic failure, run horribly over-budget, and if the director's an A-list insider represented by a major agency, he'll have a good chance of surviving, even, perhaps, being labelled a 'courageous visionary'. As far as modern-day British television is concerned, the director is a cross between a quartermaster and a bus conductor. If he has faith in his artistic vision, he's either young and untried, or a dreamer.

Tom Clegg at 71 is none of those things. He will have to deliver 138 minutes 40 seconds of action television for two 90-minute films, shot 7,000 miles from home on a 41-day working shoot, much of it in a tinderbox dry forest for which there may or may not be permission to film which is, besides, home to snakes, scorpions, wild boars and murderous thorn trees. Simulated battles will be recreated around a few untried men still to be gathered in Jaipur by a fixer, a handful of mad Russian stuntmen and the goodwill of a put-upon British crew, most of whom think early nights are for wimps while drinking is what real men do.

It is not quite clear why the Indian army hasn't been co-opted. It could be money, could be unwillingness this early on to pay off whoever could arrange it. This is the indeterminacy of India at work. No story is ever quite told – not by the Brits, not by the Indians. The official story in the

Tom Clegg takes over camera A; Nigel Willoughby stands back

production office is that soldiers disappear every time there's a spot of civil disturbance, and in this vast country of a billion people, barely a day goes by without reports of riots somewhere. But all such problems still lie ahead. This is pre-production – the 'getting to know you' moment.

At 7.30 in the cool early air, a large coach sets off for the heart-stopping ride round blind, hairpin bends up to Jaigarh Fort towering above the city. After Jaipur's humbling Indian good manners, it is almost refreshing to hear the rubble-like tones of the authentic British grumbler. Down the road at the KK hotel there was no fresh juice, no yoghurt, yesterday's fruit and unspeakable eggs. Naturally, there were sleepless nights on lumpy mattresses with hard pillows in rooms that 'only *look* clean' (this last an impossible accusation to refute).

But it isn't about the hotel. Not really. Partly, it's about who is 'valued' enough to be given one of the prized Trident-Hilton rooms, and who was relegated to the lesser KK-land down the road. Mostly, it's nerves. Only an idiot could take for granted the filming to come, when supplies are constantly being nibbled away by the 'rats' in production, to whom falls the unenviable job of safeguarding the budget, universally regarded as dangerously tight.

Hardly surprising then, that the loudest grumbles at this point come from Gareth Milne, the stunt co-ordinator. He'll be staging mighty battles, stormings, skirmishes, hand-to-hand combat using real swords, bayonets, daggers and completely untrained, mostly unfit, men. It's day one and he's pissed off. One mistake, one rotten breakfast, one dizzy head and Gareth Milne could single-handedly wipe out an entire troop. Of course he pines for the green marble bathroom and buffet banquets at the Trident-Hilton; he wants to matter to those who matter. Mostly he's remembering the days of plenty – his first jobs on *Superman*, *Indiana Jones* and *Star Wars* when money was no object, the tax system generous and work poured into Pinewood – days when he took his self-respect and self-esteem for granted.

Everyone in the business is acclimatized to months of uncertainty, wondering when or if the next job will come along. Everyone on the recce bus has done time at home, willing the phone to ring, or, for the lucky few significant enough to have representation, waiting for the agent to return last week's call. It explains the eagerness to attend all those industry award ceremonies; they serve as monuments of reassurance, dollops of appreciation. In television, belonging and being a good trooper is all.

Thus, symptoms of being emotionally needy, or even frightened, have to pop up like molehills on a grass lawn, apparently from nowhere and always in disguise. Gareth and the matter of the KK's orange juice from concentrate is an easy give-away, so too is his way of hanging back out of sight each time the recce party moves on to the next location. Throughout the day, somebody will always be looking for Gareth. He needs space, seeks almost Zen-like solace from the emptiness of earth and trees. He looks increasingly grumpy; but, more than anything, at this stage he's worried stiff.

This is the moment of truth. On board are the real players – the ones who will stand hour after hour in the heat of day, the cold of the foothills' night, framing shots, lighting impossible clearings, building forts amid scrub and desert sands. If only British trains could be run with this untiring and inventive doggedness. When interviewers marvel that some actors like to 'drink with the crew', it's usually said with the admiration once reserved for landed gentry bestowing their presence on some below-stairs Christmas knees-up. Actually, it should be the other way around.

The first of the 20 or so actors are not due to arrive for another two weeks. A welcome relief, apparently. Most crew don't have much time for 'actors'. In their view, actors are spoiled, overpaid and overindulged: 'Flighty birds, think they're magic children.' 'It's totally undemocratic. Look at what they get paid.' And, a common cry: 'Without us, they'd be nothing.' It's a rare technician who, like Nigel, the director of photography, talks of actors 'baring their soul for the camera' and the importance of trust between them. But in a way, setting up the actors as the common 'enemy' is another way to bond. By the time the stars do show up, this motley band will have burrowed into problems and, in the process, will have been forged – with one or two exceptions – into a tight, collaborative company. Without it, they'd be sunk. At the head of this company is Tom Clegg who, with his khaki shorts, desert boots, neatly clipped, balding head and gimlet blue eyes, stalks the locations like Field-Marshal Montgomery at El Alamein setting out battle order.

No one is more aware of the mission's treacherous corners than the bright-eyed, bright-faced ingénue bouncing like *Winnie The Pooh*'s Tigger among all the morose Eeyores. Dave Sutcliffe is the health and safety advisor. He does his job outstandingly well. To him, each clump of trees in the forest below the fort is a tinderbox; each smoker, a potential pyromaniac. Jaigarh Fort itself fills him with horror: there is a sheer drop onto hilly peaks, and unprotected battlements to tumble over. Everywhere he looks, Dave sees peril and menace. Black smoke? Carcinogenics. White smoke? Lung cancer. It's hard to resist the thought that joy washes over his pale New Forest face as he recognizes yet another hovering disaster, or, worst of all, some putative act of negligence. His advice has to be treated with close attention: as the fear of cholera is to overcrowded Jaipur at the bottom of the Aravalli Hills, so is an accident to a producer. Don't even mention lawsuit.

As genial and well-meaning as he is, Dave Sutcliffe has been hatched from the multiplicity of British government Health and Safety regulations, which may or may not apply in India, depending on who wants what done at any given time. Dave's tireless presence occasions the most unlikely of tirades from the increasingly grim-faced Gareth, who comes from a long, long line of circus performers – a historic metaphor for escape and freedom. 'Health and safety laws? I hate them with a passion. If they had their way we'd have actors wearing hard hats and masks on set.' A snort of derision.

'We're the only country in the world with regulations like these – do you think they do this in France? No, they bloody don't. They're just employing people to say the bleeding obvious. At the end of the day they don't take any responsibility and sometimes their recommendations are bloody dangerous. People who fucking don't know anything about this business legislate for people who've been in this industry for 30 or 40 years. Yes, I've injured myself, I've frightened myself, but I was a top-line performer and I've used my knowledge to make it safe for other people. The proof is that in all my years, I have never ever had anyone injured on a set.'

At the start of the morning, in the forest below the fort, Clegg commands complete vigilance. The crew stands to attention as he holds forth in some forlorn clearing laying out his vision of the British lines to be set up here, the ambush which will happen over there. But watch the spacing: each man finds his own small hillock or his own flat piece of earth on which to mark his territory. If another comes near, he'll move away. Sometimes the group is so spread out that Clegg's soft, winning voice can't be heard. Instead of gathering around, everyone holds his ground. Mike Mallinson, first assistant director, then booms forth beneath a stylish bush-hat. Mike is Tom's tannoy, his echo. As the hours pass, the spaces narrow. By the end of the recce, trudging through the sands of Samode, Clegg is fighting for attention as small groups form and alliances come into being. He asks tartly that there be 'no private conversations', but bonding is an important part of this outing and at least Clegg's getting brownie points for going through each location with care.

These veterans have seen it all: they can reel off a list of directors too lazy to bother with a technical recce to identify problems up front. Hot young graduates from music videos come in for special abuse: 'amateur', they say, the worst insult imaginable from pros like these. It explains why each piece of bad news is occasion for laughter, albeit black and wry. No point in complaining – those huddles are about finding short cuts, savings, miracles. As the producer, Malcolm Craddock says later: 'There's a will to see this through. They're stalwarts. There are no twitterers on this show.'

Nigel Willoughby, equine eco-warrior, languid in the Jeremy Irons mould, and director of photography, barely seems to register the implications when the lighting blow strikes at Jaigarh. This film was planned like a military campaign – actually, rather better if recent history is anything to go by. This is the last in a long line of the producers' and director's recces. In May, months before the film was financed for certain, long before anyone was hired, they flew a lighting engineer from the Mumbai hire company up to Jaipur, and brought him out to the location. He was posed three questions: could generators get through the low arches inside Jaipur fort? Was the hill on which the British attack the fort too far away for a cable run from the generator? Would the cable run to the British lines in the middle of the forest be too long for the power needed? Oh yes, he answered to all three questions. More than enough room, more than enough juice, no problem running cable down the rocky mountainside to the locations. Wrong on the last critical question.

Nigel's gaffer, Tom Gates, delivers the bad news. The expert didn't remember that power diminishes as it runs down cables. What starts off as enough wattage up there on the distant road diminishes as it drops down to the clearing. In any case, the clearing is 1,500 ft from the road and the Mumbai lighting company can only come up with cables which are 1,000 ft long. No worry at first: the forestry commission seems to have promised to build a road heavy enough to bear a truck which could ferry a generator down through the forest to what will be 'the tope', as well as carrying the many tons of lights, camera equipment and tracking lines. Tope? Some military thing, presumably: no point in asking, I might as well be invisible.

A road? To one side of the fort's entrance off the tourist coach car-park, favoured hang-out of scrounging monkeys, a path of large, uneven boulders has been thrown down for a few yards between the trees. Then it comes to a halt. That's it for road building, apparently. Neither truck nor Jeep will be able to make it any further. If Nigel was ever dreaming of an easy billet – David Lean, *Passage to India*, glorious sunsets, time to slowly put in place a string of breathtaking shots – he's long past that. Getting through, merely surviving becomes the end in itself. In another life, a director of photography might be given all the time he needs to set up the lighting for complicated action scenes. The *Sharpe* shooting schedule allows him an hour or so at most. When Nigel feels really masochistic, he thinks about that. Mostly, he shrugs and lights another of his Rizla roll-ups.

But slowly, the spell of India, the warmth of fellowship steals into the group. Wherever we are in the forest, the massive, 18th-century Jaigarh Fort, stretches to the sky in the distance. Inside one wall, 70 carpenters trucked in from Mumbai are building false stretches of wall to be stormed and breached, tunnels to be mined, jail cells to be broken out of. They are casting by hand 18th-century moulds to cover Victorian pillars and building immense cannon from scratch. Originally, the armies at the time had craftsmen such as these but it takes post-modern, throw-away Westerners a while to believe what they're hearing: the hammering and chipping of stonemasons. These are old-fashioned noises; there isn't one whining engine to disturb the stillness of the scene down to the lake at the bottom of the valley. And let's try not to dig too deeply into the ethical complications of the fact that these 70 labourers, working long hours, making everything by hand, including accommodation and food, cost less than five such men would at Pinewood.

On *BBC World* last night, Stephen Sackur interviewed a Bangalore IT out-sourcing billionaire. Watching the programme, I shuddered at Sackur's accusatory line of questioning about the way India is 'stealing' jobs from the UK and USA. Even in the Trident-Hilton's other-worldly cocoon, my heart cringed. This very fort is a monument to unequal power relations, to an Empire which stood and prospered on India's shoulders. The workers here on the battlements, building by hand, have to use skills long lost in the G8 world of plenty and technology. What elsewhere counts as recycling, here is want and necessity. They have to re-use old timber, improvise and invent – there isn't a machine tool to be had. Making do is an art form; most tool boxes hold no more than a saw, often blunt, a hammer and, maybe, a level. The workers' patience and placid courtesy is crushing. But so too in its way is today's demonstration of admiration and gratitude from Clegg and most of the crew. Who better to appreciate one set of craftsmen, overlooked and undervalued, than another?

The fort has been rented from its owner, the Maharajah of Jaipur, or, rather, from his son-in-law, the polo-playing prince and erstwhile driving instructor. Well, hopefully, the fort has been rented. As the road down the mountain attests, nothing is ever totally clear. In a country in which paper goes mouldy and disintegrates, written agreements seem to hold no more weight than a man's word carried through the air – perhaps less. There was a Silicon Valley businessman from California at Jaipur airport who caught my attention. Perfectly nice, almost affable, but he was twitching with tension. He paced backwards and forwards; his arms dangling to and fro. How on earth could anyone like that do business here without understanding that he is entering another culture, another set of 'language games'?

Match that with Alex Sutherland, production supervisor, at 34 carrying responsibility for finding locations and making them stick. The promised road wasn't built? That's life. The Maharajah's palace has been double-booked? Alex doesn't miss a beat: he scampers off to find other possibilities, while not giving up hope that the prince might be brought around. Alex started as a runner–gofer and has worked his way up the TV ladder. His were the negotiations with the prince; his the headaches, minor and major. And not once during the recce does his good humour fade, his temper turn sour. Not outwardly, anyway. It isn't easy to be the bridge between crew and production. Even less to be the son of one of the producers. Nabob handling nabobs.

There are fault lines and it's anybody's guess which will rupture first. The obvious one is generational: it can't be normal in today's world to find so many older white men in glasses still working in a major television production – at my count, most of them are over the age of 50. Compare that with the hair-tossing confidence of the 30-somethings from the production office. Another is between Brits and Indians: as the group moves around, the latter get on the bus first and sit together. Shyness? Language? For now, I assume they're stand-offish and don't intrude.

The last fissure is more subtle but tied to it: the division between crew and production, between doing and administering. Tom as director runs the recce but the man everyone looks to, albeit as he hobbles silently and painfully along, is Malcolm the producer. That this film is happening at all is largely due to his and the absent Muir's dogged determination over months, over years. A whole mountain of work preceded these few weeks known as 'pre-production'. Money (lots of it), time and tireless effort, expended without any certainty of success until the last moment. In this competitive market, getting a film off the ground is a test of fortitude, grit and faith. Malcolm can be gentle; I'm sure it shouldn't be confused with weakness.

By the time the bus covers the hour and a half journey to the desert, there's time for a pre-lunch meeting at the Samode Palace Hotel, later site of locations. Now it's Malcolm's people in production who own the floor, who sit comfortably in their skin and do most of the talking. Julia, co-producer, sits cross-legged on her chair; her voice is impersonal, business-like. She isn't the slightest bit self-conscious – or, rather, if she is, there's not a hint of it. Hers is the commanding presence and she's the one who calls the break for lunch. A delicious buffet has been laid on but already there's a vague feeling that the production staff are the hosts, the crew the guests. Right from the off, Malcolm Craddock hates my questioning him about the division – doesn't see it, doesn't want to see it. And because he's a 'good man', when the crew sit down to level with him, one-on-one, they pull their punches, invest resentment elsewhere. Besides, he may be a good man but he's also The Man: the producer is the future. He's the one who hires.

On the other hand, bouncy Alex Sutherland, all good intention, comes in for one particularly sly crew put-down. Alex is understandably pleased to have pulled off a fleet of Jeeps to be waiting in the Samode desert to cross the treacherous sands up to the various and distant locations. It's Tony from Special Effects who dryly points out that Alex's prizes are actually only 2-wheel drive disguised as 4 x 4s. Nothing in India is ever what it seems.

TAKE 3

The Director Schmoozes

At the end of a long day's technical recce under the scorching 30°C day-time sun, Gareth the stunt co-ordinator mentions that he's stopping off on the outskirts of Jaipur to inspect the first batch of 'soldiers' the local fixer is getting together. Far younger men than the director are already wilting, longing for their Trident-Hilton home and a 'dust-settler'. After complaining bitterly about the absence of any named beer known to them, the crew have immediately and happily adopted the over-sized bottle of Kingfisher as their lucky charm.

Film crews, for all their inverted snobbery, are more like a mob of public school boys than they might care to acknowledge. Just as Etonians or Wellingtonians recognize one another later in life through old school ties or stripy scarves to which only they are entitled, so crews cling to their own invented traditions, such as the Kingfisher and, surely coming soon, the *Sharpe's Challenge* T-shirt or baseball cap. There was a telling occurrence today in the Trident-Hilton lobby when Barbara Herman-Skelding, the stand-by art director, pulled up in surprise before Gareth's T-shirt. On it was printed the image of an extremely odd smile. Two alumnae of *White Teeth* in Bermondsey, London fell upon one another in Jaipur, India, and anyone who was sitting at home unemployed during the filming at the time would certainly have felt left out.

Anyway, when Tom Clegg hears about Gareth's mission, dusk is already fast-falling. With his winning smile peeping from beneath his salt-and-

OPPOSITE: *Major Dodd*

pepper History Channel moustache, Clegg volunteers to join the stunt co-ordinator, who can hardly believe he means it. Gareth's shrug may look casual but such attention from the director gives his job a leg-up in the pecking order. There have already been long, involved stories swapped about young A-list wonder-boy directors who can't be bothered with the minute details of filming because they're too busy with their artistic vision. That Clegg has been tirelessly bouncing around such outings, as well as that trip to London for the read-through, does not go unnoticed. The inference of all that energy seems to escape everyone for now. 'I like to get involved with everything,' Tom says in his blunt Lancashire accent.

Gareth's driver pulls into a field where a forlorn huddle of men wait in the dust, eyes on the constant look-out for the *Sharpe* carriage of dreams. The fixer is all spiffy clothes and jewellery. The 19 men he's turned up with are a pathetic and touching lot: a few as old as Clegg and looking decades older; a few so young and knobbly, it's hard to picture their being able to survive drilling, let alone the storming of Jaigarh Fort now only two weeks away. Gareth can barely contain his disappointment: he'd been promised 50 tough fighters. His seasoned eye tells him that what's on offer is almost useless. There follows one of those already familiar long, argumentative conversations in Hindi involving three of the Indian *Sharpe* production staff and the fixer. Immediately, faces of the would-be soldiers fall; they are crushed. The *Sharpe* high-ups turn to go – all except Clegg, who walks down the line of men, eye to eye, taking time to thank them for coming. It has all the grace and solemnity of the Queen on a factory walkabout.

'I think it's important in life to treat people with a bit of respect,' Tom says later. 'Just because they're not big stars doesn't mean I shouldn't be courteous. In my experience, if you're genuine with people, it's so much easier to work with them. Sometimes on the set the most important person is the one who's sweeping the floor. You've got thousands of pounds of equipment and people standing around and you can't turn over until that floor is clean. If I can thank the actors for a scene, if I can thank a cameraman for a good shot, why wouldn't I thank the man who sweeps the floor?'

Here's another snapshot from the directorial schmoozing calendar: this time it's only one week away from the start of filming. Tom is to make an official visit to the props shop in its concrete shell up the hill on the way to the Fort. The visit was arranged yesterday – a lifetime on the pre-production clock. Sunil Chhabra, white hair poking through black hair dye is the Indian set decorator. He and the Indian assistants have been rushing about emptying the entire contents of the props' security cage onto long tables – dishes, swords, guns, period cigarettes, powder bags, document cases, telescopes, gods, knick-knacks old and new, laid out with the precision of showcases. By 2.30, it's looking something like the Enlightenment Gallery at the British Museum. The furniture which has been commissioned and made specially by local craftsmen has been arranged outside, bullock carts have been heaved into place, sandbags stacked behind ammunition boxes. Weeks of activity have gone into this collection and everyone wants to be here to present it.

When Tom's car arrives, a swarm of Indian workers and assorted art directors fall in behind him. At the sewing machine by the pillar, one man stays at his task. He's turning Barbara Herman-Skelding's gorgeous silks into palace bolsters. Barbara, standby art director (official title), stands over him with a pair of scissors and yards of exotic cushion fringing, from which she is snipping off one at a time the gold sequins she denounces as 'over the top'. I've learned to bite back any question about such a time-wasting attention to detail before it slips out. No matter whether or not it will show on screen, I've been told time and again that the camera will know it's there. It's called 'The Look'. Obsession is the name of the game – an obsession the production people both exploit and rein in. It's a delicate and mystifying balance.

The director is led to the tables. Back at the production office, a thousand decisions wait for him. Seven days before rolling the camera and many locations are still shaky. Everyone would understand if there was a sweep of the directorial eye to reassure himself that things are moving forward, followed by a bolt back to the car. Instead, Tom works his way along the table, object by object, line by line. He picks up anything he can't make out and turns to Sunil for explanation. He holds one of the many telescopes to his eye and marvels at it. He handles with an almost sensual

"The British Army" winds through the scrub below Jaigargh Fort

pleasure the beautifully made reproduction of a French officer's gun.

Nothing escapes his unhurried attention in this small, quiet space before filming gets going. The image returns of royalty going from rivet to rivet, displaying rapt absorption in the most ordinary. A nice touch that Tom McCullagh who, as production designer, rightly 'owns' this success, instead allows the gentle, solemn Sunil to have his moment in the spotlight. Nice too that Tom Clegg picks up on it and remembers aloud that when he last made a film in India he worked with the then 20-something Sunil. It's nearly 20 years since Clegg directed his mini-series, *Lord Mountbatten – The Last Viceroy*. The Guv'nor has class.

On his gravestone, says Clegg, he'd want them to write: 'At least I tried.' It makes sense. Judging by his old-fashioned sartorial style here in Jaipur, he could probably be taken for a pallid, retired bank manager-type by casual drinkers in his local, The Turk's Head at Richmond. In India, though, it's hard to picture this zesty, energetic elf at rest. Time and again he can be spotted in the hotel corridor chatting up one of the deliciously pretty staff. He's an incorrigible flirt. 'Futile optimism,' he calls it. But he's one of life's wandering minstrels, not its predators.

It's revealing for all that. He'll try anything. When it comes to work, Tom promises to lead by flying ahead. On next week's attack on the Fort by the British soldiers, he'll be storming up that epic hill for three long nights with the extras. 'I'll be alongside them all the time. If I can do it, then they can do it.'

There's a reason that the testy Zen-master Gareth calls Clegg 'the Geezer' behind his back. He knows there's nothing this boot-maker's son from Blackpool will ask of others that he won't do or hasn't done himself first. It may not be such a blessing but Gareth has had his fill of 'flighty bird' directors who stand by the monitor and shout and scream if he delivers bad news, or seem to be pondering problems that in their inexperience they can't begin to sort out. As he says: 'Tom gets it; he's not one of those whingers saying "can't you try again" … I never confuse reticence with deep thought.'

The young Tom Clegg must have been a fire cracker. He lapped up his National Service in Hong Kong and Singapore. 'That's where I learned how to hustle and how to deal with people.' He went on to college to learn photography and his heroes were the mythic figures from *Picture Post* magazine and war photographers such as Robert Capa. In the days when companies invested in trainee schemes, ATV turned him into a cameraman. Television set the passionate sports fan to work on outside broadcasts: soccer, wrestling, church services, documentaries, news – everything and anything. At the age of 25, he was head of the camera department at ABC television. 'I was in at the cutting edge. I did *live* drama. You didn't make mistakes then – now that was truly exciting.'

It explains his style as a director: no canvas armchair and monitor for him. 'I stand up all the time we're working. I feel if I sit down, people look at me and think I'm taking a rest.' It's more than the clock ticking in his head. He moves fast not only because he has to on a *Sharpe* shooting schedule, but because it's who he is. Visceral energy bounces from him. When he works is when he is most alive. No sitting back and looking on for him. He works on the floor, stands by the camera: he wants nothing to be between him and the action: 'I have to know what's going through the camera and to see into the actor's eyes. And if I think something's wrong with the actors, I like to be able to step right up for a quiet word – not shout from 20 yards away. It's not anybody else's business.' Easy to see how and why he and Sean would get on, they are equally stubborn and private: the crew call it 'the Northern conspiracy'.

But Clegg has nothing stored up, neither money nor hobbies. His 48-year marriage has broken down and he's on his own in the suburbs. 'Life,' he says, 'has cost me a lot.' But that life has been film. For over 25 years, he hasn't stopped working as a director. No young talent coming through the system now could get the chance to end up with a CV like his – *The Sweeney, Minder, Bergerac, Morse* … he was in at the beginning of them all. 'Old age?' He doesn't skirt the implication; he's 71 and not a fool. Neither his face nor voice give away anything, but watch his sharp blue eyes. They give feeling to his matter-of-factness. 'It's going to be lonely. I haven't got a choice. But I'm not envious and I'm not covetous. I've had a rich and marvellous life.'

So if Tom Clegg's going to give out punishment in the next two months, he's not afraid to take it himself. In fact, he embraces it. 'Look at all the toys I'm being given – cameras, lights, horses, costumes, flashing swords, lovely actors saving damsels in distress. It's going to be fun.' Hopefully, this thoughtful, unspoiled man is genuinely who Tom Clegg is. The only problem is that if there is one little character flaw in a man, power will find him out. Once the camera turns, all the toys will be his or at his command. The genie has yet to emerge from the bottle.

Nigel Willoughby and Sean: the space between

TAKE 4

Director of Photography –
The Look

There's one topic mentioned a lot over the buffet breakfast in the Trident-Hilton, and that's 'the look of the film'. It's hard to fathom in this crucial pre-production phase what that means exactly, how it will be established, and how it will be made different from the previous 28 hours of *Sharpe* films.

Is a look supposed to be real and, if so, real in whose terms? Does it represent the world outside the story, a world with its own vitality? If so, India is brilliant and garish, dust-brown and dry, the sky is enormous. Will India dictate the look or is it to be articulated through and imposed by modern Western eyes, its natural luminosity stilled by good taste, rendering the country silent again under this modern-day, film-making Raj?

One thing I'm certain about: on this film, establishing that look is not so much about techniques or roles as it is about relationships. Despite the hierarchical, almost military, chain of command in film-making, who does what on any particular venture is fluid, especially on this one. Time dictates it so. On the one hand, for the Brits, it's a question of pressure but on the other, there's the yet unacknowledged fact of operating within a culture with its own rhythm. Language is use. Indians and Brits use English differently, each within their own practices. And I'm not sure all the Brits speak English with the same meaning either. It's all going to have

OPPOSITE: *Padma Lakshmi and the prized umbrella*

to be negotiated very carefully. Film unit blokes, I've already picked up, don't talk directly about what matters – not these ones, anyway. Problems creep sideways along conversations, crab-like.

It's been established that Tom Clegg isn't one of those directors who watches the action on the monitor, concentrating on the actors' performances while ignoring the bigger picture. Good news – at least, he won't be gathering a distracting crowd around himself. Monitors have a way of attracting buzzing flies like a pot of jam which is a distracting habit for a director of photography who needs space and quiet in which to create his parallel world. Bad news: instead of leaving Nigel Willoughby, his director of photography, alone, Clegg shows every sign of being the sort of director who expects to frame shots himself through the camera. There are directors who do just that, in which case they'd better know what they're doing – and be at one with their cameraman's vision. Camera operators relish the story of the hot new director who insisted on his right to choose the camera lens himself. So the camera operator produced one lens for the director's viewfinder and whipped a completely different one onto the camera. Director didn't notice a thing. Cameramen tend to worship the gods of irony.

Obviously, sorting out a relationship between a director of photography and a director who haven't worked together before is a delicate business. It explains in these early days the slightly awkward silences and unnaturally hearty chuckles in the Trident-Hilton hotel bar before supper. This is alpha-male stuff, all too easily misunderstood by intruding female crew and production staff who clearly think the gathering is about the Kingfisher beer. It explains the appearance every evening of the new-to-*Sharpe* director of photography, languid and fiftyish, who is to be found draped over an armchair with the deceptive passivity of a wolfhound. The big dogs of the set are sniffing around one another, smelling each other out.

As *Sharpe*'s director of photography, Nigel Willoughby will be responsible for creating the nature of the light – living, dead, clear, misty, hot, dark, pale, violent, subdued, poisonous, the great Oscar-winning Sven Nykvist's list of possibilities goes on even longer. Light is what creates our world; it's what gives meaning and depth to that invented one on the flat screen. Nigel spent 20 years serving as a camera operator which means that he ought to be used to being second dog.

In Hollywood, the camera operator is a technician, framing a shot exactly as directed. In Britain, especially in television, a good enough operator can function as an 'artist' while still taking responsibility for what happens physically on the floor. In composing and framing the shot, it's his job to make certain that the props look as they should, that the boom doesn't poke its way into view, that he does all his visual housekeeping. An experienced British camera operator such as Nigel expects to be left alone to get on with it, and doesn't like it much when he isn't. 'If you have a director looking through the monitor and saying "change this, pan left, tilt up", I would feel he was wasting my time and his.'

'A big screen film for the small screen' is the motto on *Sharpe's Challenge*. Translated, that means not enough money, not enough time, not enough anything. It's ambitious film-making on a locked and limited budget. The television film business is young, but still old enough to have in its collective memory a golden age – an age of security, BBC and ITV trainees, enough men on the job with time enough to do it properly, or enough wastage to have men standing around doing nothing. Like *Rashomon*, everything depends on the point of view, where you stand or, more correctly, where your own interests lie. As director of photography, Nigel is here to establish the overall look, as well as being the film's main camera operator. 'It matters not a jot to me what they call me. I love what I do but I can't be precious about it.'

In big enough films, the DOP doesn't operate. Why wouldn't Nigel want to bring in someone else? 'This kind of production can't afford the people I would trust,' he mutters darkly. He's skirting the issue and being slightly ironic, but the usually patient Malcolm bristles. I've touched his Achilles' heel. 'Not everything is about money, whatever the crew who don't understand it all, may or may not think'. On his last three projects, the DOP has always operated the camera because Malcolm believes strongly that if one man lights the shot, frames it and then shoots it, the result hangs together better. But that's Malcolm: in today's television

The cannon: hand-built at Jaighar

business, too often that's life on money grounds alone.

What is true is that Nigel trusts himself to capture on Camera A the way he wants the shot to look. He's also aware that amid the 600 or so members of the British Society of Cinematographers, there's still a debate about the rights and wrongs of this kind of two-for-one. In the talking shops of London, perhaps it's an old-fashioned British demarcation issue: it's about jobs, and saving them. But underneath, for men like Nigel, there's a familiar and more fundamental sense of loss: television no longer needs artistic vision from its cameramen.

Watch any regular drama series or soap and see how catch-all lighting floods and flattens everything and everyone. Letting loose a cameraman such as Nigel who can compose a frame as a painter does a canvas, light with chiaroscuro to illuminate each particular drama, is a delicacy. It's something for the special occasion, a treat such as *Sharpe's Challenge,* but too rich food for everyday. And anyway, who needs it? 'I'm one of 600 cameramen and most people wouldn't tell the difference.' He isn't bitter, he's sad. He's mourning an artistry disappearing under the brutalizing influence of high-definition video and competitive costing. Budget woes in television today are like malaria in Jaipur – endemic and increasingly resistant. It's why the shooting schedule is so tight even on an 'event' enterprise such as this.

There's a clutch of problems Nigel hasn't even spotted yet. The director has had as much, if not more, experience operating the camera as his DOP. I've already seen the way Tom likes to 'be involved' in everything. Tom Clegg is an action man from sports and outside broadcasting: get in, get on and get out. It's how he managed to deliver all those early *Sharpe*s. 'No one but Tom could have done it,' goes the ominous phrase time and again.

Nigel Willoughby has a sensual, almost dreamlike, quality about him. He shies away from putting his own vision into words or even talking about camera work in general. 'I don't tend to look at other people's work. I like my lighting to come from the heart.' But with time, he talks of his heroes, about the way excellence inspires him: Vittorio Storaro and *Apocalypse Now,* Freddie Young and *Lawrence of Arabia,* Philippe Rousselot and *La Reine Margot,* anything lit by Chris Menges or Roger

Deakins. Beauty is what drives him.

He longs to deliver the real India to the eye, to hold onto the special quality of the air around Jaipur. Its haze diffuses the light, softens it, gentles the contrasts. But capturing beauty takes time. 'Bear in mind that we have a schedule which is almost impossible. We're shooting two films in seven weeks. Television's getting sillier and sillier every year. You just have to soldier on.'

Soldiering on does not mean interferers are welcome unless, that is, they are one of the great directors of photography or directors, many of whom Nigel has worked for. Almost his last job as straight camera operator was on *Portrait of a Lady* for DOP Stuart Dryburgh and director Jane Campion. He's a shy man and finds it hard to let show his pride in the way he captured Campion's vision of the dark, seductive complexity of Henry James. He's done two pictures for Antonia Bird and before *Sharpe*, had come off a French film with yet another woman director, Lisa Azuelos: 'Language is no barrier when it comes to film – it's a telepathic experience. Anyway, I love women directors,' he says with relish. 'I love the way they want to reach for the soul.' It's the first real hint of the emotional mêlée behind his 'just one of the guys' facade.

Here is a dreamer who fought authority all the way through school and went out into the world at the age of 16. The film unit turns out to be full of such dreamers and rebels. 'My father sat me down and said "You're on your own now, I can't do anything more for you. But I'll give you one piece of advice: you're too honest for your own good. It won't work in the world out there." He was right so I'm usually in a minority of one.' His estate agent father was, according to the son, a rogue and an idealist: 'I've got the same genes only not necessarily in that order.'

Perhaps that's why he spent so many years as a camera operator not aspiring to move on up. 'Ambition doesn't drive me. I've seen so many who get to the elevated heights and something happens to them. They become impossible. "I'm an *artist* – I have to have everything now."' He took on a director of photography position only after Stuart Dryburgh pestered him until he agreed to lead the second unit on *Bridget Jones' Diary*.

Why hadn't he wanted that extra responsibility and input earlier? He's obviously a man with a strong vision of his own. At first, he's defensive: 'There are great cameramen who stay in it for life. That's why they tend to be laid back – they've seen it all, all the bullshit, all the egos.' This is a man who writes poetry in his free time, who lands with delight on the latest Paulo Coelho novel in the bookstore, but he's also a pirate who has taken years to reach some kind of peace with himself. 'I was lazy and I fought shy of the challenge. It took me a long time to realize that not trying something was as much of a failure as trying and failing.'

Somewhere out there on location is Nigel's mate, who's got six months to shoot a major feature film. A truck goes everywhere with him, crammed with lights and equipment. If Nigel dreams in India, it's of having lighting cherrypickers towering high over the Jaigarh fort walls to do justice to them in the black night. At this point, he'll settle for lights. Period. 'I've never been able to do my best work. In television, it's always a compromise.' Brits take a reverse pride in calling themselves 'technicians' but it's just a way to disguise hurt. 'The crew are always on the bottom', is a familiar cry.

Probably as a result, TV soldiers, especially in Britain, don't tend to the snobbery about equipment which all too often surrounds feature films. Panavision, for example, is to cameras what Blahnik is to shoes. They're especially favoured by American studios because they're thought to give a slightly glossier look than Nigel's camera of choice – the Arri. The Arri (formerly known as Arriflex) is German-made and robust and, in Nigel's book, every bit as good. A tough, reliable camera is what he asks for – it's the lenses which make the real difference for him. 'Cameramen play lenses very close to our chests.' The better they are optically refined, the more chance he'll have of sharpness and clarity. At one point, *Sharpe* was going to be shot on 35mm film; cutting back to Super16mm makes it £100,000 cheaper. Even so, Nigel's planning to use 35mm lenses. He wants the bigger expanse of glass to capture and process that special Jaipur light more quickly.

Next week he hopes to test some filters before shooting starts. 'I'm probably going to use antique suede colour-correction filters. They err towards the sepia but they'll subtly give us a little more contrast without losing this wonderful diffusion.' He'll have an agonizing wait before being sure it's worked. The negative film will be hand-carried by courier to London for processing, transferred to Beta tape and then directly digitized for editing. Not only will he be watching rushes five days behind shooting, he'll be watching them in his Trident-Hilton room on DVDs. 'Film is an organic material,' he laments. 'When you digitize the look, you flatten it.' To a purist like Nigel, it's anathema.

He comes from an era when the cameraman's achievements were more nakedly up there on screen – as were his mistakes. Modern technology has not only stretched the parameters of what can be done but also of what can be got away with. Nowadays, if a director of photography makes mistakes – doesn't quite match a scene, hasn't matched the light, the contrast or colours – it's easier to overcome with digital grading. But old-time pros prefer to do the work with their own eyes. The camera is their window and through it they paint the drama.

Drama, however, is something Nigel understands. His own emotional life has in its time been something of a train wreck, as have the lives of

Nigel, DOP

most of the *Sharpe* men. It's all that intensity hidden away behind the façade of soldiering on, of hail-fellow-well-met. Almost no one here is what he appears and the stories of wild affairs and broken marriages are legion. Calmer waters at last, says Nigel: 'I'm a free man now. I'm old enough and confident enough to think people employ me as much for who I am as what I do.'

He may say so but next year he's taking off to South Africa to help build a house for children with AIDS. 'I have to start doing something that makes a difference. I've never been able to cope with the paradox of all this – the contradiction between the pointlessness of what I do and the humanity out there.'

Age may have brought him confidence but it has brought humility too, which is as well. He talks with passion about the weeks ahead. 'Tom Clegg's job is the drama, the performances of the actors – mine is India.' My mistake is in mentioning this to Tom Clegg, 'The Colonel', as Nigel has already nicknamed him. The director bristles. His is the framing, his the composition, his the film, he asserts with pique. It's not *Nigel's* camera: the camera belongs to the show.

The dogs still have some sniffing to get through. But the Director of Photography will surely find his own way around The Colonel. After all, Nigel's such a softie that he once got on a dodgy plane simply because his lighting gaffer Tom told him he couldn't imagine a nicer man to die with.

Karan Panthaky as the touching Kande Rado – and the Maharajah's umbrella

TAKE 5

The Art Department –
Dressing the World

Money. It has become the constant topic of conversation, of bitching and moaning. And yet no one wants to say – except under a vow of confidentiality – how much their budget is, let alone how much they're getting paid. Such topics are treated with a dogged secrecy in a situation where there are no secrets – except for the one about money.

A detour, but it's still about money. It sort of supports Malcolm's point that when it matters, it's spent. Film labs exist in India – there's one in Delhi half a day away – but *Sharpe's Challenge* rushes are to be hand-carried to labs in London by two couriers working in rotation. Rushes are all there is. If they're lost, they're insured, but the mess is still catastrophic. Filming ends a few days before Christmas. Actors are contracted to a specific date – would they stay on for re-shoots? Losing the film is the ultimate production paranoia. Sending it to Delhi to process wouldn't save the ultimate terror – the long trip to London to the editor and post-production. Irrational it may be (Muir certainly says so – and loudly), but £15,000 is found to pay the couriers. And no one will sleep easily until the film is processed safely in London and transferred to Beta tape on which it will eventually be cut and transmitted. £4.5 million and all this effort reduced to one small black box, as if that isn't in itself irrational.

Anyway, it's unusual to be told almost at once that the Art Department

OPPOSITE: *Sharpe goes undercover in enemy territory*

has a budget of £160,000, of which £75,000 is for construction. The information comes – admittedly, with the sums wrong – from Tom McCullagh, the Production Designer. He's direct, with a soft Belfast lilt which doesn't harden no matter what. It's why, in this already emotionally-charged and labyrinthine world, talking to him is one of the pleasures of the day. His sentences are simple, his meaning clear. He's modest, so much so that at one point I ask, only half-jokingly, how on earth he sold himself to his agency, PFD, which has one of the most glittering lists in London. 'There's no point in jumping up and down and saying "I can do this. I can do that." At the end of the day, it's based on work. I was brought up that way. I'm just level-headed about most things.'

He arrived in Jaipur a month early to start recreating India in India. Not a 'real' India, but an 'authentic' India. The difference? Clear as mud. One involves the world out there in the past and present, in the crowded bazaars and emporia, in the sumptuous palaces. The other involves the art department's library of British academic reference books and a search for rooms and furnishings which either never existed, don't exist or exist in the wrong colour, shape or shade. Tom, as usual, is clear. Authentic means an object captures the essence of the period; real is an antique and it costs. So, for now, in my mind anyway, 'authentic' is shorthand for money.

Tom's Look also grows from his reading of the script. When he came to design the desert fort yet to be built at Samode, he focused on sad, pitiable Major Crosby, posted in a place no one would want to be. From Crosby's written scenes came Tom's vision of a fort, weatherbeaten, sunbeaten, desolate at the end of a nowhere valley. But once you start thinking of the image as content, seeing a film set as a metaphor for the action and emotions of the story, obviously who designs 'The Look' involves yet a third, complicated set of relations.

Tom McCullagh wasn't the original choice; another production designer was on the job before him. True to form, he doesn't prickle at the reminder. I suspect he knows that at first glance he looks too ordinary and sounds too unassuming to defend his artistic ground against the indefatigable Colonel and the yogi-like director of photography. Tom has still blue eyes and a face like a round, ripe apple. There doesn't seem to be a temperamental streak to him. 'I'm not about making a scene so the producer can see or the director can see. It's just the way I am.' Meanwhile at 43, he's represented by PFD, while the director who used to be with that same agency has now chosen to represent himself. It's a telling discrepancy which will be rubbed home when the full unit list is circulated. These are not small matters.

Tom's deceptive appearance explains the somewhat unflattering amazement as the brilliance unfolds of his design and solution for the false wall at Jaigarh Fort. Originally, the wall was to be built up against the existing fort, set back behind a cobbled road. Two problems: first, this left no hill at the top for the British troops to storm in a suitably dramatic fashion. More important, shortly after filming starts next week, the script calls for the wall to be blasted and breached. Obviously, you can't blow up the real fort and no one came up with a solution, until Tom was brought out to recce. He wandered about by himself for a few hours, and sketched his solution straight onto paper. He simply moved the wall forward down the hill. The building terrain was better, his wall abuts the steep slope and the cobbled street behind creates the mined tunnel. Hey presto, three for the price of one.

Seventy Bollywood carpenters were bussed in from Mumbai and it is they who are building the massive 30ft wall and turrets. Of the four weeks allotted to its construction, one was lost waiting for permission from the Maharajah who owns the fort. Indian time has its own pace and what Pinewood would knock up with a kit of electric tools, is being built from start to finish by hand. 'When I arrived and these guys were holding a piece of wood with their feet and doing it with a hammer and a saw, I thought: "Stuff that, this isn't going to work." And then I came back and saw what they'd done. I had to eat humble pie. Who am I to judge these people?'

Tom's humility turns out to be rare; 'shout louder and it'll be done faster' is the customary Brits' response to another culture's way of life. No surprise, then, that the designer from Northern Ireland is one of the few Brits to co-opt his Indian crew fully into his team. He trusts Muneesh Sappel, his Indian Art Director; he incorporates him, as he has Sunil. Tom knows about outsiders and exclusion. He was marked by growing up

Catholic in Protestant Belfast during the worst of the Troubles, albeit with parents who guarded him well. 'If you had morals, you'd have to be disgusted or shocked. But keeping my feet on the ground, it's just the way I was brought up. We were always taught to be straight in our dealings in every sense.'

He was one of seven children of a labouring foreman who dug trenches for the post office. 'He was secure in the sense that as long as you were fit to do the job you were secure.' Tom wanted to ditch school at 16, but his father wouldn't let him. 'He'd come home mucked from head to toe. He didn't want that for any of us.' The hard, early years show in the way he stands firm, without throwing his weight around. They show in the way he deals with the tensions of pre-production. No cavalry swords? Wrong guns? Walls not finished? 'Yes, there are problems but there are also solutions' is his quiet answer. Above all, they show in the way he has held on tightly to family life and how his flat voice softens when he talks of his wife and three children. He's made it clear that he's flying home to Belfast a day early. No matter what, he's going to be at his daughter's first nativity play. No one even tries to change his mind.

Tom McCullagh draws strength from his roots – unusually so in the film business, if this unit is anything to go by. Most of the men have been cut adrift by the discontinuities. The talk is of what happened in Romania, what a pleasant surprise filming in Argentina turned out to be, of Bulgaria and Borneo. Odd that no one seems to make the connection between their adventures abroad and the demise of the industry they love in England. Hollywood goes where it's cheap. Forty years ago, that was Britain, but no more. That's not the only price. It's hard not to notice how many of the older men turn out not only to have grown-up children, but also babies and toddlers with new, younger wives. And even harder to overlook the fact that none of the bright, high-achieving women on *Sharpe's Challenge* have children at all.

It's never easy to work out from unit titles who does what on *Sharpe*. The Art Department has one production designer (Tom), two art directors, three assistant art directors, a standby art director, a set decorator, two assistant set dressers and an assistant buyer. Several of these seem to sit about in the props room half-way up the hill to Jaigarh. One or two mill around in the production office, which has set up in an apparently abandoned hotel, round a muddy corner from the Trident-Hilton.

Film people learn to perch and nest where they land. On Tom's office wall in the production office, his assistant Henry's beautiful architectural drawings are hung, and the wardrobe has been adapted as an ersatz gun safe. If there is 'A Look' to *Sharpe's Challenge*, most of it came out of Tom's head. It's been his vision since he came out on that first recce. He talks of wanting authenticity which isn't the same as accuracy, of wanting not what *was* real but what *seems* real. Once upon a time, period drama meant escape into an artificial past. One era's furnishings melted into another. Long dresses and wigs spelled history. Period drama nowadays has to smell of reality – but a reality acceptable to the contemporary eye. In India, that's complicated.

In this land of red sandstone and dry brown soils, 18th-century rulers celebrated wealth with colours brighter than jewels – they were an announcement of power. In *Sharpe's Challenge*, Tom's look for sets and costumes is more muted, more Armani than Rajasthan. Brilliance, when it

Tom McCullagh with cavalry stunt team

comes, will serve the drama not the history books. 'This isn't a documentary.' Viewers these days are thought to be visually sophisticated: modern drama, like modern life, is about signals and communication. How Tom communicates that post-modern thought to all those art directors isn't yet clear.

On the wall outside his office hang four large brown envelopes for notes and letters. They're neatly labelled – Tom, Barbara, Henry and Sunil. Here's the clue to Tom's kitchen cabinet. Sunil, the newcomer from Delhi, has the face of a medieval martyr. 'He speaks from his soul,' Tom says of him. The other three met in Slovenia working on a badly-judged *Heidi*. They console themselves that it looked good and they had a great time together. When Malcolm Craddock turned to Tom McCullagh, he in turn co-opted Henry Harris, a slightly more cheerful version of Victor Meldrew, and Barbara Herman-Skelding, standby art director, throaty, blonde, Scouse and beneath a seriously neglected haircut, the face of Ingrid Bergman.

Titles mislead more than communicate. Barbara is responsible for dressing the sets. What she calls 'boys' things' – swords, knives, bayonets – she hands over to Sunil. Thus, when the cavalry swords promised days ago don't arrive, it's Sunil who knows to choke on his apology. 'I can't have people who are intense,' Tom has made clear. 'I can't have people who take the drama, and triple it.' Barbara's worrying shows in a different way – her attention span whittles away to seconds. By the time she gives her answer, she's forgotten the question.

Barbara Herman-Skelding isn't a list maker; she carries a thousand details in her head. It's not as if there are regular office meetings to help everyone catch up and stay on message. Organic is how Barbara describes the way it works. TV on a budget is a curious mixture of DIY and professionalism. Set dressing is no easy option on period drama. Hers is the responsibility for what she calls 'soft' stuff but today alone includes the Maharajah's sumptuous palace, the Duke of Wellington's library and an entire army camp. As for bullock carts, campaign tents, tea chests and the like, the men in the props store are busy making everything from scratch.

This is Barbara: she has a repulsive-looking fungal infection in her mouth, swollen glands, temperature and assorted other aches and upsets. She'll show her crusted, ulcerated tongue to anyone who'll look. She won't take time to go to the doctor. 'I've never missed a day's work through illness' is her proud boast. When she finally agrees to fit the clinic into one of her famous shopping adventures, she keeps putting it off while we dip in and out of silk shops in the crowded city market, and she stops to hold involved conversations with begging children ('My, your English is good. May I congratulate you?'). Barbara Herman-Skelding is merry and fearless. On the wall above her desk is a notice which reads 'Strange man Barb has gone off with', and an address no one could find even if they needed to. 'Vikas (Rinku). Behind Patwar Sangh' could mean anything.

Most of the Brits go out on forays together and preferably, with an Indian crew member to translate. Those who've 'done' Romania, et al, know better than to expect anyone to speak English. The elegant Brits from the costume department never go out alone. No production car available? Barbara goes off by herself in whatever taxi or motorized rickshaw presents itself. Nose twitching, she'll set forth in search of the ultimate chair, the right table or the perfect brass dish, no matter which back alley it leads her down or which shopkeeper knows somewhere better to take her. 'I'm forever going in cars with strange men and I never feel frightened.'

Nothing much rattles Barbara – nor has it since she left home at 16 for a weekend in Amsterdam and kept on going until she got to the Lebanon. 'My parents weren't too chuffed.' For years, she had a series of what she calls 'shit jobs' – bar work in Teheran, lambing in Scotland, bus conducting in Devon. 'I never thought I'd have a career, I just did jobs to earn money.' It's a cry all too familiar from and to women. Somehow Barbara ended up managing cinemas in London, with the Electric in Portobello Road on her patch. Watching films in rep, sometimes 12 each week, she fell in love and, with her usual enterprise, put up a notice at the Film School at Beaconsfield offering to help students with graduation films. Bingo, she was an art director.

It's that same imaginative energy which propelled her to pop videos, then drama and, now, the recreation of an 18th-century world, thousands of miles from home. No hiring props' houses in Jaipur as she has in London to fall back on, no familiar contacts: everything's an adventure. Going with her to find the embroidery shed in which young men from distant villages have been charged with hand-beading the maharajah's umbrella, is a typical experience: 'I know it's a right turn along here somewhere – I think that's it, oh no, maybe the next one.' One road leads to a mud lane, to an even muddier lane and an unlit concrete shell in which men sit embroidering jewelled beads onto a stretch of exquisite, gossamer-thin material. It's breath-taking. It's not even worth asking how she found it.

The Maharajah's Umbrella, like the Maharajah's flag, has become 'a saga'. There's always some prop which runs amok and brings out demons. The youthful Maharajah is to be represented by a particular shade of turquoise. With difficulty which can hardly be exaggerated, Barbara has found the right turquoise silk. The umbrella maker by appointment to the present Maharajah of Jaipur holds court in a small cave tucked into the busiest street in the old city which is below the palace and almost impossible to reach. Unfortunately, the umbrella maker has his own ideas about style so can't be trusted artistically to adapt to 'The Look'.

No one wants to explain that to the Maharajah's umbrella maker, his father, uncle or grandfather, all of whom are present and cross-legged on the floor, bewildered at the carry-on. Barbara has rootled out the right silver handle but isn't prepared to accept the umbrella-maker's ready-made and appliquéd beading. Hence the hunt for the hand-beaders in the back of beyond. Once they have hand-sewn each bead onto the turquoise silk, Barbara will take it back to the umbrella-maker to fit the silver handle.

One more detail means going back again to the beading shelter: Barbara wants to see the gold sewing thread. It mustn't look too new, can't be shiny. Please find a new thread with the feeling of old. Can this really matter? Is it worth the time? I'd go almost anywhere for Barbara's company but we've been away for hours. Will anyone notice sewing stitches? Or even the umbrella? 'It's all in the detail,' says Barbara, and in her sunshine voice is the rumble of thunder.

Henry's paintings for the Duke of Wellington's library is another such saga. It's worth recounting. For all I know at this point, maybe beauty and skill can and will transcend the underlying values they depict. Let's not forget that this is not Jane Austen but a film about bloodshed, killing and power relations. In an early scene, Wellington summons the reluctant Sharpe and orders him to India. Unfortunately, there are no paintings in Jaipur that even approximately match those in Apsley House, London W1.

So Henry Harris, on what might pass for his own time were it to exist, did sufficient research to find out that Wellington owned paintings by Goya and Velasquez. They were captured after the battle of Vitorio and gifted to him by King Ferdinand VII of Spain. On the National Gallery website, Henry identified and ordered reproductions by the same artists, got someone from the London production office to collect them, and someone else to negotiate world rights for 10-years unlimited use for digital, terrestrial, satellite and cable television worldwide. They were then hand-carried to Data Reprographics near Shepperton Studios for Bubble Jet printing onto 7 ft by 5 ft artist's canvases, which were brought out in someone's hand luggage from Heathrow via Delhi. Barbara bought lengths of appropriate wooden framing in Mumbai and carried it back to Jaipur. She and Henry made the frames themselves and mounted the canvases late one night. Will the three paintings be on screen for more than 10 seconds?

There's only one man who can control Richard Sharpe, only one man he fears – and that's the cold, manipulative Duke of Wellington. Let's assume that there's some sign or texture that these paintings can convey which transcends words alone. Even if we don't know how Wellington got them, the paintings could speak directly to us of power and supremacy in war. It's what directors call 'a moment' – an indispensable, emotional moment of truth. If the moment doesn't happen, it was a seriously big waste of Henry's time.

Henry doesn't much care. He's not a frightened man because he's seen worse – his recent bill from the Inland Revenue for £30,000 for instance. Somehow he hadn't caught up with paying for the years of plenty. He cashed in his film industry pension ('it turned out to be not very much anyway'), and has already paid down his debt to somewhere £3–4,000. It's left him without a credit card, which is tricky in a foreign country. 'I was frightened at 50. I'm not worried now.' Yet another of the *Sharpe* men approaching retiring age without financial security.

It doesn't stop him from speaking his mind. 'Our director thinks *Sharpe's Challenge* is all about "boys' stuff". It's not. It's not just down to guns and bangs and crashes. It's all the ideas Tom comes up with, all the stuff he designs that seems to grow organically from the sand here, all the stuff Barbara does …' But in the new *Sharpe*, will there be room for the quiet stuff to make its impact?

The make-up trio: Marc Pilcher, Marella Shearer, and Tori Robinson
– known to the Indian crew as Medium Sir, Big Madam and Little Madam

TAKE 6

The Countdown

Storm clouds gather four days before shooting begins and it's no fun at all. In New Delhi, terrorism. In Kashmir, after the massive 7.6 earthquake, political wrangling over the sick, hungry and homeless. There is an interesting divide between those on the unit who fret over their own problems but keep apologizing for such solipsism, and those to whom there is no world but the film set and the Trident-Hilton. It's as if for the latter group, celluloid is their only reality. These are the people to avoid in the last few days of pre-production: their drama is *the* drama. Their intensity is exhausting. They drag themselves home at night, noticeably later than everyone else. In that most public of spaces, the hotel breakfast room, they make a point of seeking Garbo-esque isolation.

The unit troopers don't appear to notice these silent-screen heroics but it comes out in digs that are dark and sly. They seem to be funny and sympathetic, but it's also a way of testing me. Will you repeat them and make mischief?   Are you friend or foe? Can you be trusted? These are the unasked questions rolling around the hotel bar. Journalist beware: here are lions and tigers and bears.

The crew have almost all met somewhere sometime before: there isn't one of them who arrives in Jaipur as a complete unknown. They've looked one another up on the internet, and checked out anyone they don't know personally by word-of-mouth. If you've made enemies or weren't liked on another shoot, the industry family will pass it around. And if all else fails, they'll judge one other by the carry-on, or absence of it, under the pressure of crossing the last bridge before battle.

It doesn't sit well with the Kingfisher set that Sean Bean didn't get into his Upper Class Virgin seat on Sunday as booked and is still in London. His mobile phone is switched off; his whereabouts unknown. People want to know that three days before the first day of filming, the leading man is here, getting used to the midday heat, getting fit with the attendant sword master – mostly just being around. He's the money. 'Scared off by the bombs in New Delhi,' jeers one. 'I told you. He's petulant,' warns another. 'He's private, he's shy. He doesn't want to sit around not working,' offers a loyalist. The point is this: without Bean, none of the other cliff-hangers matter. He's not the only actor to be late to turn up. So too is Salman Rushdie's exquisite wife, Padma Lakshmi, cast as Madhuvanthi, the Indian equivalent of the Queen of the Night. No one even noticed – except the frantic costume department when she took against her frocks. No, the fact is that Team Bean wants to matter as much to him, as he does to them. And of course, they don't – that's the rub, that's the hurt. His absence belittles them.

Meanwhile, problems unravel. For the first time, there are meetings behind closed doors in the production office. This is when the topic of money comes out in the open. No coincidence that this is the day when people start confiding to that they've taken a third or even half of their usual fee; how everything in television is now done on a shoestring. The rumour goes round that someone in charge is getting a bonus – 10% of every pound sliced off the budget. Money is always a symbol of something other than itself. Here, it's one way the troops have of winding themselves up before going over the top, deep-down scared that they won't get the problems sorted in time, won't meet *Sharpe's Challenge*.

Here are a few of Monday's problems. Richard Bonehill, sword master, who's been travelling all day and night from his home in Cornwall to Jaipur, gets to the prop shop to try out the specially-made weapons, Sunil Chhabra's particular pride. Clearly treading on eggshells, Richard hardly knows how to begin. He could, probably should, have brought swords out from England, but he didn't. Although he can cut through the air himself with what's on offer, he can tell immediately that they are too heavy for thespian arms. This isn't guesswork. He'd been granted a few hours' rehearsal time with Bean and Toby Stephens in London. Are they fit and in shape? It's a question this mild-mannered fencer doesn't want to address. Sorry, he says, the blades need to be made of aluminium not steel. Poor Sunil hardly dares to breathe as he waits for the manufacturer beetling in on the road from Udaipur. Watch carefully but there is no overt sign of this sweet, dignified man's tension. Tomorrow is the Diwali holiday, bigger than Christmas, Jaipur is feverish with excitement: what hope has he of new swords by Thursday?

At this point, all humour is black. Henry Harris compares getting stuff done over Diwali with the time he worked over Christmas at Shepperton reconstructing the execution cell from Wandsworth Prison. A lesson quickly learned: never interrupt a good unit story with detail. It doesn't matter why. 'A hanging? Better than my usual Christmas,' finishes the lugubrious Henry. This is prompted by a query as to how close to being ready is the false wall for 'the breach' at the fort. Clearly, not quite.

Tom McCullagh and Barbara Herman-Skelding are already up the hill at Jaigarh dressing sets for Thursday's shoot. They've finished the rugged tavern newly created from a hole in the wall. Tom has had some clay hanging lamps made, to which I'd paid no heed. The design came out of his head. If you don't notice them, he says, they're 'authentic'. Got it at last. Almost ready is the sumptuous Maharajah's loggia on the parade ground where the Mumbai labourers have recreated stone columns by hand and a period roof to camouflage corrugated iron and old drainpipes.

Unfortunately, the monkeys which usually live in the forest are captivated by all that's going on. For the first time in years, they've moved back into the fort. For a few days, they sit in long lines on the walls and battlements weighing up the action and planning their strategy. They're bright and full of fun, and, clearly testing the waters, have taken to using the newly-erected catering tent roofs as their trampoline. No one's afraid of human thieves because there are 24-hour security guards. Fortunately for everyone's already rumpled peace of mind, they have yet to be seen – each one turns out to be a sweetheart, and most are well past retirement age. But all those inappropriate jokes about monkeys ripping into Tom and Barbara's sets, disguise deep unease. If anything symbolizes the fragility of control freaks, then it's the monkeys' defiance of order.

Monkeys are sacred. Even shouting at them brings disapproval. Gareth the stunt co-ordinator, who deep-down prefers animals to people, hasn't helped by chucking bread to them. One morning, Barbara throws an old breakfast banana to a band in the car park: the next woman to open a handbag is leapt on with frightening enthusiasm. Even while this is going on, someone has to tell the story about the assistant director who was bitten by a monkey with rabies, helicoptered out almost immediately, and still hasn't been able to work years later. She's lucky to be alive, he says. Thanks for nothing.

The best stories on offer are in a canvas 'workshop' strung up on bamboo poles built against a hole inside the fort wall. Tony Auger, special effects supervisor, his face gaunt, his silky, greying hair already drying out with stress, is on his second packet of Silk Cuts in an hour. His tall, brawny side-kick Garth Inns is chain-smoking Benson & Hedges. Everything that could go wrong already has, or so they think.

American rocket engines? Don't even mention the fatal word 'rockets' to the edgy Indian authorities. Not a hope of bringing them into the country. The steel mortars in which to set explosives can't be welded together because there isn't a welding rod. No matter, no explosives as of now. Napthalene for black smoke? Nixed by the production department on safety grounds. Even before the Delhi bombings, India was on high security alert. This is hardly the moment to try to import enough mortars, explosives, fuses, bullets and gunpowder to blow up a city and a series of impregnable forts. Tony's entire shipment has disappeared into a hole somewhere in customs. The outlook is bleak.

Gerard Naprous, the horse master, has been in jail for the last two weeks in Udaipur. He'd gone on a recce to find horses but, on the way back, the Indian Airlines' airport X-ray machine turned up two rounds of something explosive at the bottom of his briefcase. They must have been there for months, left over from another job. Of course, it doesn't pass notice on

Black Monday that no one had spotted them at Heathrow. Draconian laws govern airline security in India: they specify no bail, and mandatory prison sentences. No horse master and no Udaipur horses. Here's another of those character litmus tests: who minds about the missing horse master, who minds more about the missing horses?

Hoping for inspiration or a miracle, the two special-effects wallahs are lolling in chairs, taking 'a whinge break', while Tony keeps a doubting eye on four Indian workers painstakingly making bullet hits by hand, an uncertain and lengthy procedure. They've made action films in India for years but their technology is 20 or 30 years behind Britain's, let alone America's which is where Tony buys his stuff. 'They make enough films in the States for there to be a market for pyrotechnics and where there's a market, there's a manufacturer.' The sun is climbing overhead and even in

Rocket Hill: Tony of SFX chain-smoking, David Higgs, 3rd A.D. behind him

his dandy Alpine hat, the 18-stone Garth is sweltering. Monkeys have already bounced enormous gashes in the canvas roof. Special effects is at a virtual stand-still. Ten labourers were promised for 8 o'clock this morning to move huge canisters of gas. It's after 12 and Tony and Garth are still waiting for them.

To cheer themselves up they've fallen back on that old standby: swapping stories of even worse disasters. Garth kicks off with trying to cross the border in Syria to get stuff into the Lebanon. Driving through snow in Istanbul and over gorges in Greece, custom officers who tore apart their special effects and dismantled guns without being able to put anything together again. Then they start on pet hates. Garth's is method actors: 'They're such a pain. They take ten minutes to wind themselves up. They live the character and won't come out of it even in the evening.' He remembers having to build a plastic fridge because one actor had to be able to punch in the real thing, or it couldn't happen for him. As Olivier is said to have suggested to Dustin Hoffman: 'Why don't you try acting, dear boy?'

Tony's pet hate is the lighting cameraman who's been through film school, knows all the theory about key lights and side lights, and nothing about anything. 'They want to light rain from the front. It looks like a curtain. You have to light rain from behind and the side so light comes through the prism of raindrops. Then you've got snow and you've taught them about rain, so now they light snow from behind. If you light snow from behind, it goes black. You light rain from behind and snow from in front. Of course they never want to be told anything, so sometimes the only way is to kick over a light. "Oops, how did that happen?" It's been done before.'

When they get really desperate, they resort to the worst disaster of all: the imminent demise of the profession they love. 'I think we've got ten years at the most before computer generated image takes over,' says the doleful Tony. 'Once their libraries are big enough, they won't need us any more. The insurance companies will say: "Why have risky explosions next to major artists when you can do it on computer?" The only reason we've survived this far is because CGI is mostly in the hands of computer nerds so a lot of it is still rather naff. Once people with some artistic sense get into it, they won't need us any more.' Time for lunch, and that one about what happened when Garth drove from Taif across Saudi Arabia and on into Afghanistan …

Ciggies and stories are what keep film units going; they're the real food and drink. Marella Shearer, the voluptuous make-up designer, all heavy silver jewellery and unruly dark curls, is already up to 40 Dunhills a day. Her make-up and wigs, amputated stumps, severed heads, blood and wounds, absolutely everything, are stuck in customs in New Delhi and haven't yet been cleared. These are not dangerous explosives so the rumour mill has it that production is still haggling over import duty. 'I suppose you can work around not having sashes, but I don't know how you work around no hair and make-up,' another toss of those wicked curls. The costume department is in a mad panic ripping apart and putting together uniforms for the various armies, hundreds of uniforms. They were a job lot from another film: alas, with the wrong coloured collars, cuffs and buttons. They look authentic enough. In the costume universe, apparently, only 'real' will do. But that is still to miss the point: in the chain of film-making, tailoring bends the knee to make-up.

Marella's trunks will clear tonight is the promise from the office; they'll be driven up from Delhi and get here tomorrow. Fat chance of anything happening on Diwali, say the wise-guys. For lack of anything else to do, Marella holds court over a pot of tea at the Trident-Hilton and tells stories of needy luvvies. '… anyway, I couldn't get her out of my chair. Then she throws her arms around my waist and says "tell me you love me". I nearly popped one out and fed her.' Actors: always good for a laugh in a tight corner.

No one laughs, though, when word goes around the Trident-Hilton lobby: Sean Bean didn't get on the plane today either. I'm reminded of something he said to me late at night in a London pub, when I first met him months ago,: 'I'm not a fucking robot,' he spat out in response to some imagined slight. 'It's bloody scary when you sit in the trailer on the first day of starting work and you always think: "Am I going to be able to do that?" It means so much to you; it's such a wonderful thing to be able to do but it's scary, it's fucking scary.' Getting on a plane was the first step towards the *Sharpe's Challenge* Number 1 trailer.

But then I remember the wolfish grin as he added: 'And then gradually you get more confident and become a fucking big head.'

The fort's monkeys drink from the honey-wagons

Shooting the Stars

After years of working to finance Sharpe's comeback, weeks of pre-pro-duction and three days in which Bean's assistant was left waiting in New Delhi airport, Muir Sutherland and Malcolm Craddock sit in the deserted Trident-Hilton lobby at 6 am, two warhorses past retirement age, savouring the victory of having got this far. It's the first day of shooting: 322 bits of scenes to go, 789 different set-ups, 41 days to do them in. Their film is seriously under-funded by most accounts so if they're jubilant, they're also savvy enough to know that troops need chiefs who ooze con-fidence.

Last night's football game serves to get the two producers into the car and up the hill to the fort. 'Manchester United lost,' Muir is gleeful. 'I hate the arrogant bastards.' The only team he hates more, it seems, is Chelsea, mostly to do with traffic jams along the King's Road when they're playing at home. Various hairpin bends up to Jaigarh are spent reminiscing about the night 21 years ago when together they watched their beloved Spurs bringing the UEFA Cup Winners' Cup home to White Hart Lane. Anything but talk about the day ahead or express thankfulness that their star finally showed up. 'Oh, of course he was going to come. He's really keen,' says Malcolm, really meaning it. By now, Malcolm's face has shrunk back into his skull. Every bit of flesh he doesn't need has been burned off. This man knows he's taking a gigantic risk.

There was relief all round at the sight of Sean Bean working the hotel

OPPOSITE: *Toby the ultimate professional*

restaurant last night. He kissed Marella Shearer the make-up designer, who fluttered and blushed. He awarded firm handshakes and gave eye contact to everyone who mattered, and then sat down at the toffs' table: Muir, Malcolm, Tom Clegg and the gorgeous Padma Lakshmi. It was a great performance and took nerve after turning up three days late. Had he bunked off for room service, no one would have blamed him. This very public dinner had the impact of some dissolute young prince's repossession of his abandoned court – and so grateful were nobles and commoners alike that they overlooked the prince's matted and striped hair, and the black circles in his ashen, ransacked face. Marella lit up at the challenge. 'He'll be *gorgeous* when I've finished with him.'

It is still dark when the catering tent opens for breakfast and nervous attendants in white gloves lift silver tureen lids to display eggs, bacon, baked beans, white toast, an array of Indian dishes, fresh fruit, Tetley tea bags and unspeakable instant coffee. Despite this last, it's an impressive beginning.

Catering tent A has red rugs carpeting the fort floor, brightly-patterned cotton tablecloths and wall-hangings of vibrant Rajasthani prints. The food has to be cooked miles away in Jaipur and rushed up in trucks. Supply lines are all. This is a film about war. Armies march on their stomach. So far, so good. The courtly Indian catering manager stands at the entrance to the tent, personally thanking everyone for coming. It is a flourish of old-world manners. It bodes well, so too does the azure sky and extraordinary dawn light breaking over the Aravalli Hills.

Film crews make a point about not being superstitious. It's a way of distancing themselves from actors who are deeply so. As Bean's opening night success in the hotel dining room demonstrated, the relationship with stars is complicated. Anyway, crews *are* superstitious. How the first day of shooting goes is regarded as 'a sign'. Everyone is on edge, and pretending not to be. Bad sign that shooting has had to be re-arranged to accommodate Sean's late arrival. He was meant to be the opener: throw in your big gun first. Another bad sign that the photocopier broke down last night and the production staff were up late, laboriously printing out the revised shooting schedule page by page from their laptops. If they're lucky, they'll get through four pages of the script today.

'At least we won't get rained out', says the lugubrious stunt co-ordinator, Gareth. Rajasthan has been desperate about the lack of rain for years but it's a blacker joke than it appears. Rumour has it that there's no weather cover, given the expense of insurance. Although you'd never guess, Gareth is on a bit of a high. His daughter had a half-English, half-Indian friend at boarding school whose parents live in Jaipur and are close friends of a Rajput who owns polo ponies. He's not only agreed to provide all the horses the unit needs, but has helped to recruit 'soldiers' for Gareth to train. His one condition: Gareth takes an equal number of underprivileged young men as private school sports' stars. His demand pours honey on Gareth's troubled social conscience.

At 6.50, the drift starts towards a small terrace overlooking the valley rifts. Here the gentle, young Maharajah of Ferraghur and his tender-hearted sister will play the first scene of the shoot. It's unfair. The actors are young, nervous and unknown – sufficiently unknown and powerless to have been bumped off the Trident-Hilton Hotel list and put out of town at the KK. (Be sure that didn't happen to the imposing Mrs Rushdie.) But they are touched by a moment of inspiration. The sun is coming up through the mist and the light is pure gold. A flock of birds sweeps across a boundless sky. Nigel Willoughby stands lean and high above the crowd on the camera dolly. With his long hair washed and flowing, he's as still as a carved figure adorning the prow of a sailing ship. There's a shy sweetness in the way he turns to the director and in a voice warmed through with feeling, calls out: 'good luck, Tom'. A partnership is being forged; it cushions the young actors and they respond to it.

Everything else leads to this moment. Three hundred crew, seventy carpenters, workshops employed all over Rajasthan and, in the end, it comes down to a few words on a page and two young untried Indian actors. They are fairytale figures – he in white silk and she in a floating and embroidered dress, the lining of which was the subject of a day's hunt through the teeming bazaar in the Pink City. Too peach, too gold, too yellow, too pale, too dark, too shiny, not shiny enough: bale upon bale of silk unfolded in sari shops, large and small. Finally, late in the afternoon, exactly the right silk was run to earth in a small, windowless room at the back of a long, second-floor corridor above Sarogi Mansion on the Military Road. It couldn't have been harder to find or look less promising.

Contemporary drama may get away with one fast raid on Selfridges but period pieces must bring out the worst compulsive behaviour in costume designers. It leads to a particular sort of controlled hysteria: think shards of ice, think thin, think Anna Wintour of *Vogue* magazine. Just to walk into the costume department at any time is to catch a dose of tension. Whereas the art team had reached out to and co-opted Sunil, a deep schism was already apparent in pre-production between Sujata Sharma, the rounded, chain-smoking Bollywood 'Costume Supervisor (India)', and Claire Anderson, 'Costume Designer', fortyish, pointy-edged alumna of Birmingham University, the Royal Opera House and Wagner Ring Cycles.

Claire may come over as Cheltenham Ladies' College but she's a work-ing-class girl from North Yorkshire, a lethal mixture of tough, perfection-ist and fragile. Her assistant, Katherine Burchill, a purist organic vegetari-

Make-up trio

an, is having a food problem, looks more rake-like by the moment and takes to cooking her own omelettes in Catering Tent A, to the astonishment of the caterers and amusement of the crew. I finally brave the costume shop with an offering of a bottle of ProGreens with Advanced Probiotic Formula, courtesy of the Kitchen Shrink in Devon. Claire's response to the intrusion sends me scuttling out again.

The two of them, almost always clad in black, dart around the costume shop at what must seem to the Indians like the speed of light. They have 2,500 costumes to get ready during this production. 'That's nothing; I had 7,000 on *Seven Years in Tibet*,' Sujata offers, perhaps an attempt to reassure, perhaps not. When the list was circulated of those supplied with local mobile phones by production – another mark of seniority – I had already picked up that Sujata's name wasn't on it. And, perhaps in retaliation, a remark of Claire's about people who sit at desks all day smoking is made in a stage whisper, and does not pass unheard.

So when the Indian tailors don't turn up on set on this first day of

Garth Inns putting blood bags into costumes for bullet hits

shooting, it becomes apparent that communication in the costume department might have broken down. The problem is compounded by the fact that the exquisite Padma Lakshmi is still upset about her costumes and now about her make-up. Madhuvanthi is crucial to the story; Mrs Rushdie is going to be crucial to *Sharpe's Challenge* publicity. It was unfortunate that, because of her grandfather's death, she flew in late to Jaipur, otherwise the problems with her costumes might have surfaced in time to do more than despatch the director to reassure her.

Between Padma's concerns and the absence of alteration tailors, the shooting of her scene has to be put back for an hour until the ever-indefatigable second assistant director Ben Burt is able to locate the van of tailors and send it steaming up to the fort. Meanwhile, Padma picks her way back to her trailer from the make-up tent, an eager assistant holding over her head a huge striped golf umbrella. What a find for whoever managed to unearth that.

By comparison, Sean Bean is the trooper sent by the gods when he finally gets to work. He's out of his trailer before he's wanted, on set, patiently standing by, as good as the gold he's earning. Unit rumour three days ago put that at £500,000. The state of the betting on Sean's fee is a good barometer of the current mental health of the crew. The greater the fears, the more they have to be trodden down, the higher the suspicion about how much their star is earning. But shooting has started, the first scene has gone well and almost everyone can handle the pressure. Currently, Sean's thought to be earning not a penny over £400,000.

In the parade ground, Gareth the stunt co-ordinator is trying to turn eight slight Indian men into vicious killers. They perch on a wall in the shade of a tree, their arms around each other, watching in delight as Gareth demonstrates the simple sword routine. Again and again, he tries to drive into them their mantras: 'If the sword travels, your body travels.' 'Below the waist, the sword is always down; above the waist, sword is always up.' One by one, they take him on. 'Don't grip the handle. Keep your hand soft'. 'It works better with three fingers than with four.' On and on he goes, his voice unchanging. Considering the danger these heavy weapons pose in the wrong hands, his patience is remarkable. He's firm but manages to keep the atmosphere light. 'What's all this swathing about? You're going to lose an ear.'

Suddenly, Gareth switches tack. The lovely Buddhist turns into smouldering evil, he howls and swings his sword as he advances with venom on the unfortunate young boy opposite him. It terrifies everyone. As suddenly, Gareth stops and gives his earnest, hangdog smile. Point made. Backs straighten to attention. 'I hate action films,' Gareth laments over a lime soda. 'They should be shoved down the toilet. It would get rid of all the egos, all the bullshit. It's just gratuitous nonsense. But I've grown into that opinion or I would never have got into this industry in the beginning, would I?' Age may have brought Gareth understanding and principles; but a lifetime has been spent honing skills which contradict both. It's one of life's ironies: it is the gentleness and harmony that he loves most about India, and here he is trying to beat it out of these Indians.

Meanwhile, on the opposite corner of the parade ground, sword master Richard Bonehill is working with the eight Russian stuntmen. This is swashbuckling stuff. They're fit and athletic. 'Tough doesn't do it, I'd rather have a ballet dancer,' says Richard. 'Fit and athletic, that's what you need.' The Russians, veterans of all the early *Sharpe* films in the Crimea, are lunatics, everyone knows that or at least hopes they still are. They're mostly in their 50s now, and everyone registers that too. Of course, hardly anyone knows that Oleg was a theoretical research physicist until it stopped paying – or anything else about them really. They're always referred to as 'the Russians'. It's assumed they're morose and immune to fear.

'I am afraid every time. It's normal. If you are not afraid you are stupid,' Oleg says later. They like to work; they hate to hang around. So when they're not working, much of their nervous energy centres on drinking and, unfortunately, they've had to be left on their own at the Diggi Palace Hotel. Its aristocratic owner, provider of the polo ponies, has already expressed concern that the Russians have been drinking openly in the street. It's a serious, criminal offence in conservative Jaipur and he worries that they'll be arrested. 'You must stop them.' 'Stop them drinking?' Gareth repeats in disbelief. No one wants to take that one to the Russians, let alone believe it could be successful. And, of course, there is another drawback to the Russians: they're not Indian. They can't be allowed to die in the foreground during the storming of the fort. Gareth's tender young Indians have about three days to be turned into ferocious stuntmen. Or at least taught to fall onto mattresses and die convincingly.

Elsewhere in the fort, it's business as usual. Marella's 40 litres of blood have been lost in customs. 'How can you have battles and no blood?' Tony's welders now have a rod to seal the mortars, but they can't use it because the generator noise which powers it can be heard on set. The loo in the specially installed Western toilet wagon doesn't flush; the monkeys keep drinking from the water tank. Jaigarh Fort is a tourist 'must' and the Indian security men are too soft-hearted and polite to keep families away from the set, or to tell children to pipe down. A party of American paying guests of the Maharajah are lunching and chattering on the parade ground, their round tables decorated à la Martha Stewart. It's an odd juxtaposition to the grunting Russian stuntmen.

In Sean's trailer, stains have been discovered on the carpet, and dust on his Sony DVD player. Two men have been drafted in for cleaning detail. A driver has been despatched to Jaipur to buy a second pillow for Sean's trailer bed, and told not to come back without one. And if there is a contradiction in the way the actor is treated as Little Lord Fauntleroy and the way people complain at him being spoiled, there is never a good moment to bring it up.

Some things are going better than expected. Outside the fort, the indefatigable assistant locations manager has trucked in enough rocks and sand to make a last-minute road down to the inaccessible forest clearing. Does he have a licence from the Forestry Commission? He reaches into his pocket and pulls out a thick wad of 100 rupee notes. 'This is my licence,' he says. 'This and 131.' From the other pocket, he pulls a packet of 131, the local cigarettes. His road builders think it's terribly funny.

Best of all, today's filming has an enchantment about it. Tom's art department turned a neglected hall into a temple full of light and colour, of hanging brass lanterns and clouds of marigolds. It looks over their ultimate triumph – the fort gardens where newly planted trees and flowering shrubs now lead the eye to the misty hills beyond. An empty concrete trough has been intricately painted to match the temple and filled with water. Such is the beauty of this place, the sight of doughty Henry scattering an entire sackful of rose petals on the water is just too much. It touches my heart. 'It'll smell nice, anyway,' says Henry, followed by: 'I doubt anyone will see it.'

TOP: *Malcolm's twice daily visit to the set, with Sean and Daragh*

BOTTOM: *Daragh and Sean: Harper always stands behind his man*

TOP: *Lucy takes cover*

BOTTOM: *Gareth Milne, stunt co-ordinator (left) and the Rajput, Ram Pratap Singh: soul brothers*

TAKE 8

Actors Are Different

It is five o'clock on Sunday morning, the fourth day of shooting. A 4x4 sweeps up the last rocky bend to Jaigarh Fort, waking the night watchman. Ram Pratap Singh, Rajput, royal and lean, 46, masterly veteran of the Rajasthan Polo Club, owner of Diggi Palace and its hotel, has come to inspect his 16 thoroughbreds and stable-lads. The former were spotted and bought from racetracks in Delhi, and are now officially on loan to *Sharpe's Challenge*. The latter come from one of his villages out in the desert. His forefathers owned a kingdom of 240 villages; at least 500 men in what's left of his kingdom would still die for him. It gives a certain commanding security to his gaze. It's a long while until dawn but his boys have already fed the horses, which are pawing the sand in the temporary bamboo and canvas stables built for them in a deserted corner of the battlements.

The night air bites at the top of the tall escarpment and one of the horses has already caught a cold. The stable lads, who slept on the ground by their charges, report the news phlegmatically; they'll have her well by lunchtime. These men have passed their lives with animals. At 2 and 3 years old, they were out in the desert, in Diggi village, herding goats in the fields, their food for the day wrapped in cloth. From goats they graduated to cows and, finally, the village's precious buffalo, so when Rajput Singh handpicked them to work in Jaipur, these fast, temperamental, sinewy beasts held no fear for them. Taking note of the three reconstructed fingers

OPPOSITE: *Daragh as Harper, British spy*

on the Rajput's hand, I feel grateful that he doesn't expect outsiders to go anywhere near his horses without his nod. Before he will entrust them to any of the actors, he insists on personally giving riding lessons to all of them out at the polo grounds.

As a result of these lessons, the slim, austere Rajput with his piercing dark eyes, is now something of a racing tipster. He knows, for instance, that Toby Stephens as the traitorous British officer, Captain Dodd, is scared but that he will seem to ride down the precipitous cobbled hillside for the camera later with total aplomb. As indeed, he does. Pale, but haughtily in character. His is already a villain to treasure.

Nor is the Rajput surprised to hear that Sean Bean doesn't show up for filming today. He is sick in bed, presumed to be the effect of last night's supper of tandoori and chips. The Rajput's invitation, stiff with royal insistence, that the actor should come out to the polo fields to be matched with the right horse had already been deflected with careless charm and mutterings about there being no time.

The Rajput is keen on what he calls 'real'. Life in his villages is 'real', the teeming city is not. The organic dairy he runs in the garden of his Jaipur palace is 'real', so too is his conservative family with its educated, warm-hearted women. When he was in his 20s, the Rajput ran away from his responsibilities and went to hang out in the film business in Bombay. Film and actors? Unreal, of course. But of *Sharpe*'s leading actors who've made the trek through the grid-locked Pink City (actually, more peach than pink) out to the polo field and its 16-hole golf course, the one who embodies most closely the Rajput's virtue of 'real' is Daragh O'Malley.

The shambling, 6 ft 2 in Irish actor played Sergeant, later Sergeant-Major, Harper, Sharpe's faithful 'chosen man' through all the early years, and has returned for the *Challenge*. For Daragh, the Rajput handpicked Asher, a big powerful mare from Calcutta, clever enough to make herself unmanageable for polo but affectionate enough to become his children's ride. In his judgement, the shrewd, pleasure-giving Asher will be safe in Daragh's large and generous care. Two chancers together. Without knowing it, the shrewd Rajput has hit on the core of this Irish actor.

O'Malley's character, Patrick Harper, devoted his years with

Wellington's army to Richard Sharpe. He protected and saved him; he risked his life to watch his back. He was both messenger boy and saviour, a huge, hovering presence without too many lines of dialogue. One scene from episode 2, *Sharpe's Eagle*, tells all: the wounded Sharpe is desperate to capture Napoleon's standard at the Battle of Talavera, and Harper carries him there through the thick of fire and smoke. The feat makes Sharpe's military career. *Sharpe*, of course, made Sean Bean's career. It funded his divorces and children, and eventual success in Hollywood.

Sharpe funded Daragh O'Malley's move to a Hollywood of pilots that never got picked up, a course on the Motion Picture Process at UCLA, and a convoluted business deal in Dublin with Patrick Duffy of *Dallas* which ended horribly but somehow resulted in Daragh getting £250,000 from a British tabloid to settle a libel case. No, it's too complicated even to recount and, as a matter of fact, he says he took home less than his lawyer by the time the latter had deducted commission and costs. It's a typical Daragh coda. Even more so is that he went on to lose every penny of his settlement in a spectacular Irish production of *The Rocky Horror Show*.

It's the story of Daragh O'Malley's career, as it is of so many actors, notoriously careless of themselves. The actor's life is lonely, isolated and boring for most of the time; acting becomes 'life' and alcohol flows through the cracks between parts. Think of Richard Harris, Peter O'Toole or Richard Burton. It's about 'the guys' and about insecure lives in a zone which permits, encourages, even forces them to be irregular. All pleasures are based on whether or not they're working, and without the hunger to work – almost a disease in itself – they don't make it. Daragh O'Malley is one in a long, distinguished line of actors who hurt themselves as much as, if not more, than they do others. So all his stories promise the inevitable ending of a scorpion's tail.

Take the time he was hired as the voice of the horse in an animation blockbuster. He was replaced because his horse sounded morose. Then there was the time he took his earnings from three years as the Irish gardener in the soap opera *Crossroads*, and invested it in a picturesque old property in Ireland. In it, he opened a take-away restaurant, Up All Night, a cake shop, a slot machine arcade and a betting shop, Marine

Bookmakers. This last, meant to underpin the lot, haemorrhaged money. 'I must have been the only bookmaker in Ireland to have lost my bollocks.' Then, when he hadn't got round to paying the insurance premium, the whole place burned down. 'So it was back to work and a lot of years just melted away.' Another cigarette, another shake of the large, jowled lion's head.

Daragh doesn't just give away facts about his life; each one is a wandering tale. It involves at least a packet of 20 Rothmans in the warm Indian afternoon, the reciting of poetry and the speeches of men shot for the Irish cause nearly a century ago. His stories, which may or may not be true in detail but are always so in spirit, roam across Ireland, taking acting lessons from Marlon Brando, from Beverly Hills to Raglan Road, Dublin. It takes time to see a pattern in the disaster and tragedy with which each tale ends. It is the emblematic Irish actor's life, or at least fits the stereotype. There's a mean irony to it: here is Daragh who embraced Los Angeles, still misses it every day and for whom every opportunity went wrong, or led nowhere. There is Sean who clung to Sheffield and Hampstead, and yet works

Daragh O'Malley as Harper:
a monument to friendship

steadily in Hollywood, a town which gives meaning to the saying 'out of sight, out of mind'.

Except, right now Sean is neither there, nor here. He's in his room at the Trident-Hilton having injections and solicitous concern. And Daragh O'Malley in his LA baby-pink sports shirt with its collar up just so, is not being dragged behind a fierce Pindari horse up a cobbled back lane to Jaigarh Fort today. Instead, he's hanging around waiting for Chelsea v Arsenal on the hotel television and, later tonight, playing in the Caribbean Poker Classic final. He's made it through to the last 30 and has every expectation of taking the $3 million prize. It's so real to him, he can almost touch it. Mostly, he's waiting for Sean to call him. Had Daragh the strength of will, he'd probably have kept to his decision to turn this job down when it was finally offered.

Sean Bean went pay-or-play on *Sharpe's Challenge* on 1 September. From that day, he was entitled to his full fee whether or not the film went ahead. As Daragh remembers it – which is not, of course, as anyone else does, but can as easily be what happened as didn't – it was almost the last moment when anyone remembered to call Daragh's agent. The date of 23 September is branded on him. And the call came with an offer less than he was paid for the first *Sharpe* 12 years ago. 'It was an *insult*, an insult.' He had long since heard of other parts being cast, long since been emailed the script by another actor. Acting is a small world: good friends pass the word quickly, bad friends even more so. He knew Harper had been written in. Of course he asked himself whether someone else had been signed for his part. That's actors. That's absolutely Daragh.

In the end, he couldn't hold out, if he ever intended to. Chances are he believes that as he remembers it, everything was actually so. This is a man who overflows into life; it isn't in his nature to be measured, disciplined or calculating enough to turn down *Sharpe's Challenge*. So he's been a woeful figure around the Trident-Hilton for the last week. He arrived when expected, eager to go, and spent his first three days in Jaipur waiting. Waiting to hear from the second assistant director when or whether Sean would arrive, waiting for Sean to pick up the phone to him, and, deep down, brooding over a far longer silence. 'Five years I lived with Sean and the read-through in London was the first time I'd seen him in nine years. *Nine* years.'

Everything's personal for Daragh. He's surrounded by ghosts: the other actors who were 'killed off' at Waterloo or before, memories of laughter and camaraderie in the Crimean, Turkish and Portuguese trenches where almost all the first 14 episodes were filmed, of the days hanging together on set before Sean's breakthrough trailer.

A betting eye would probably have put more money on Daragh than Sean before *Sharpe*. He was the son of Hilda Moriarty, the Irish beauty for whom Patrick Kavanagh wrote 'On Raglan Road', Ireland's great poem about unrequited love. His father was Donagh O'Malley, Fianna Fail Republican MP, political voice of Limerick's poor, excluded and dispossessed, government minister, president of the Football Association of Ireland, alcoholic and compulsive gambler who died of a heart attack at 47. He must have been a Titan: by the time Eamonn de Valera made him a minister, he'd already caused a scandal by ripping up a statue of GK Chesterton and smashing open the Irish Parliament doors with it in a drunken rage. As Daragh tells it, that is. But he's also the man largely credited with setting free the Celtic Tiger with his revolutionary introduction as Minister of Education of free primary and secondary education for all children in Eire.

As a father, he must have been terrifying in his unpredictability. Limerick taxi drivers actually refused to take him when drunk. After one such refusal, he hurled a brick through a shop window, stole a bicycle and cycled home. But he must also have been magnificent and imaginative – for his son's eighth birthday, he presented him with the services of a carpenter to build a stage in their four-car garage. Opening production: *Francis of Assisi*, all seats sixpence.

The grand 18-bedroom, 27-acre Victorian property in Dublin had to go after his death, of course. According to Daragh, his published estate cited one premium bond and a greyhound. It didn't mention the £38,000 bank overdraft and gambling debts. His mother, who hadn't practised medicine since the day she qualified, needed to work and retrained as a psychiatrist, specializing, perhaps predictably, in alcoholism. So Daragh, her pet, graduate of four elections' canvassing for his father, was packed off to Terenure College in Dublin, first as a boarder and then as a day boy, lodging alone in Mrs Frehill's B & B. He was 15 years old.

He wants to tell the story as a *Boys' Own* adventure: all soccer successes and girls on the streets of Dublin. It's almost a party piece and about as convincing. It's hard to imagine the damage done to the gifted young boy who suddenly lost his larger-than-life father, was sent away by his mother, and life as he had counted on it simply ran through his fingers. As it has, more or less, ever since. Sometimes, though, he lets through a perplexed hurt. 'What choice did I have? My father was a big-time alcoholic and gambler. And on my mother's side? Gamblers and alcoholics.'

Two years at drama school in London, the second as a star at the then 'hot' LAMDA, an agent and work soon came his way. Three years in the soap opera, *Crossroads*, theatre at the Mark Taper in Los Angeles, and a long spell as Ireland's most successful (and only) actors' agent – same story, really, making it work for others, losing it for himself. The Beverly Hills adjacent apartment behind Sunset Strip which he could have bought for $275,000 after the big LA earthquake? It's now worth $2 or 3 million; he didn't buy it.

His biggest break of all came a decade ago, playing a humble Irish fisherman and leading man to Debra Winger in a film co-starring Johnny Depp and Marlon Brando. It folded after four weeks' shooting when Orion pictures went bankrupt. The day it collapsed, he remembers more with dark surprise than bitterness, Marlon 'fucked off in a taxi to Shannon Airport.' It cost Daragh £31,000 to settle unpaid bills in the tiny Irish fishing village location. 'It was like a stake through my heart. I asked Marlon what would happen to those poor people. He said they'd all end up in the Home for the Bewildered.' If he notices any connection with his father's debts, he certainly doesn't mention it. He's on a Marlon riff, awestruck at the friendship with his god of acting, amazed that when he had to hold Brando's hand for a scene 'it was shaking, he was so fucking nervous. I gave what I could by take 3. Marlon got going around take 12. *Marlon Brando* was fucking nervous.'

The final irony, as it happens, is on Sean Bean, not O'Malley. Sean has ex-wives and children, pressure to keep running, to keep earning. For

Bean, stardom has to be about always moving forward. Daragh's Irish wife, Gabrielle, runs a highly successful property company in Dublin where they now live. 'Why did I leave LA? Every single day I miss LA but I didn't want to end up like one of those sad, fading English actors looking in the bargain wine bins at Trader Joe's.' And yet here he is again, seeing the ghost of the young O'Malley coming round the corner, praying that *Sharpe*'s rerun won't turn out to be another of his disasters.

'I started *Sharpe* when I was a bright bushy-tailed 38-year old. Why am I here? I'm now 51 and for the first time in my life, I have a life. I have my wife, my dog Paddy and my parrot Vincent. I'm not grieving for the life I haven't had, believe me.' Would he be any different had there been children to anchor him? Probably not. Intelligent, giving, warm and self-indulgent, he hurts himself more than others, and certainly laughs at himself first. He's like a very oversize man buttoned into a suit too small.

At one point, he recites the words of Padraig Pearse, shot by the English in 1916. With them he won a National Public Speaking Competition as a young boy. He remembers it all and it's a spine-tingling O'Malley moment. One phrase, though, lingers through the Indian dusk: 'A fool shall laugh in his hungry heart.'

Late in the night, he plays his final hand in the Caribbean Poker Classic. And loses.

The Orion film that folded was *Divine Rapture*, or rather, it would have been had it been made. Daragh was in the confessional box waiting to confess to the priest, Marlon Brando, that he'd committed adultery with the local hairdresser. Brando had decided not to talk to the actress Debra Winger. '"There are three sexes in life," Marlon told me, "male, female and actresses".' So Brando had co-opted Daragh as his best friend and they were chatting away while waiting for the camera set-up. 'You have a fucking unique ability and I have it too,' he told the Irishman. 'You can walk into a room with 35 fucking people and in five minutes you can pick out the three or four who don't like you.'

It's probably an exaggeration to say that Daragh O'Malley idolizes Sean

Bean but he certainly craves some of the magic dust of being liked by him. It lends poignancy to what happens in the next two days. For all the idle conversation when they sit together on set at the end of the first week's shooting, Sean doesn't seek Daragh out. In the same way the producers, in his mind, took it for granted O'Malley would be available to play Harper and in the same way Harper watches out for Sharpe, Daragh's eyes are on Bean first, not vice versa. It's the curse of the profession. It seems to be personal, but in the end it's business. No one's fault, but a man like Daragh with no clear boundaries will inevitably be hurt. It explains why the profession is a Minotaur, gobbling up young actresses, but that comes later.

By the sixth day of shooting, which is the end of the first week, Sean is back on set for the big swordfight scene with Toby Stephens as the traitorous Dodd. This has to be complicated for Sean, with 'outsider' branded on his wiry, chipped Yorkshire shoulders. It's probably not so much that Stephens was born to theatrical royalty, the son of Dame Maggie Smith and Robert Stephens, as his tasteful, gilt-edged career. He's 'distinguished' rather than famous. From Sir Peter Hall's *Camomile Lawn* to *Cambridge Spies* about Philby, Burgess and Maclean, his television appearances have been 'prestigious'. So too his films: Orsino in Trevor Nunn's *Twelfth Night*, Lensky to Ralph Fiennes' *Eugene Onegin*, Neil Labute's *Possession* from AC Byatt's intellectually virtuosic novel.

The stinger, though, is his stage career: its chattering-classes' success with the Almeida Theatre in Islington at its most chic, and in productions transferred to and fêted at the Brooklyn Academy. He's done the whole leading-role Brit thing at The Royal Shakespeare Company, capped by his *Hamlet* last year for Michael Boyd's first production as artistic director at Stratford-upon-Avon. Compare that with Sean's *Macbeth* five years ago, which, as one interviewer spitefully put it, was praised by a third of the critics. Besides, Sean's Shakespeare was put on in a commercial theatre on the Strand, not the right cachet. It isn't that Sean hasn't had his RSC chance: it picked him up soon out of drama school but it's part of his complicated 'outsider' stance that he despised its elitism, even though he craves success.

The swordfight takes place on the parade ground. Way in the background, the watchful Daragh, aka Harper, stands for hours in front of lines of uniformed Indian extras. Seated in the sumptuous loggia – a mouth-watering zinger from the art department – are the young Indian Maharajah of Ferraghur, his sister and, as the British General's captured daughter, Lucy Brown, a 26-year-old Oundle public school graduate and star of the Guildhall School of Music and Drama. She's playing Celia, the English rose and damsel in distress, invented to be rescued, hair pieces galore tumbling over young magnolia skin.

Lucy has a natural sweetness; she doesn't throw herself around, doesn't only talk to the men who matter. Padma Lakshmi, erstwhile model for Ralph Lauren, Ungaro and Ferretti, can't help but outdress and outshine other women at gatherings and parties. She's gorgeous, that's all there is to say. Lucy, lovely, open and unaffected, makes a point of dressing down, of blending in; everyone likes her. It's not her fault that she's playing a part guaranteed to turn the stomach of any hard-working woman on the set, fighting to make it alone in a brutal industry. But even though on paper 'the romantic lead', Lucy is a supporting actor; originally she had been posted to the distant KK hotel until Tom Clegg gallantly insisted she be moved into the Trident-Hilton.

Lucy's casting clearly delights the elfin Clegg, bouncing around the set, trying all at once to direct the actors and frame the shots. He doesn't seem to notice Nigel's long fingernails drumming on the camera department box, nor does he consider that he might be irritating his director of photography each time he takes a peek through Camera A, while shouldering the heavy, hand-held Camera B himself. Tom's like a desert warrior on a blitzkrieg, and dressed for the part in his usual shorts and boots.

There are lots of edgy situations on set today, not least the competitive clash between the two leather-booted actors swaggering in testosterone-soaked, see-through shirts, accentuated between takes with spray-on sweat from the Junoesque Marella. One of the delights of the day is the sight of Marella in gold-threaded panama and generous cleavage holding court with Tori, tiny blonde rock-chick and Marc resplendent in black vest and tattoos under striped woolly trilby. I understand now why the Make-up & Hair department has special status – it's the only crew allowed to touch the flesh. The front-row presence of Marella's trio is filming's version of knitting by the guillotine. Only make-up ever knows the whole score.

Richard the sword master and veteran sabre champion, number two in the UK, five in Europe, eighth in the world, has choreographed a vicious, clanging and complicated fight which has to be pursued while exchanging a long and crucial dialogue. As far as possible, it has been broken down into abbreviated sections to be shot one at a time. Even so, it means turning at exactly the right moment, on exactly the right spot, while delivering exactly the right line. Toby Stephens is fired with an energy which, it might be supposed comes in some part from the fact that filming has had to be re-arranged around Sean's indisposition, leaving Toby to fly out late tonight to take in an important meeting tomorrow in London. Meanwhile, Sean is all affability, displaying an unusual on-set camaraderie while swapping jokes and experiences with the tall, erect Toby. Thespian competition bristles about the place, much enjoyed by the laddish element of the unit. 'It's like cockfighting,' says Malcolm Craddock appreciatively.

To recap: Sean arrived looking gaunt and scraggy, his looks redeemed only by Marella's wizardry. He's been sick and laid-up in his room. If he's been working out at home in London, it doesn't show.

Alistair Crocker, the owl-like production sound mixer, sits on his upturned box by the portable mixing deck, trying hard to work out what that is. He's been in this business for over 35 years. To while away the boring bits, he's even been trying to make a list of the films he's worked on in his tiny, well-behaved handwriting. He can't remember a whole slew of them. He can't even remember clearly which was the year he made *The Full Monty* and *Mrs Brown* as well as a *Harry Potter*. Anyway, he listens intently to Sean through his headphones and ignores the way the star often mutters incoherently, fluffs and can't get his lines, and he starts to put together the different ways Sean has of stressing words, the way he goes under them, changes inflection, throws some away, softens and colours his tone.

Toby is the more clever actor. He's worked out that the aluminium sword blades will give headaches to the post-production sound mixers because they don't have the 'ring' of steel. Each time he has bits of dialogue following a sword's clash, he waits for a vital second or two. In 'gapping the dialogue so beautifully', as Alistair puts it, he'll make it easier for each sword stroke to be cleanly cut out and replaced. 'Such a clever actor,' says Alistair approvingly. 'Very, very professional.' I listen through the headphones and am awed by how dependable Toby is. He articulates loudly, playing to the distant Maharajah; drops his voice exactly when required to Sharpe. If there's an occasional American twanging vowel or missing consonant, Alistair lets it go. 'We're not working in splendid isolation, you know. The sound has to act on the conditions of the picture, and we need to be diplomatic and realistic. I don't want to be some bloody person coming in and saying "don't do this" and "don't do that".'

Something is nevertheless happening that goes far beyond clever and professional, and it's coming from Sean. Even the wise and experienced Alistair can't explain it. There's no reason for him to be indulgent towards the star. He too was sick and of course he turned up on set regardless. 'Well, you have to don't you? Filming is about discipline and endurance. You're allowed to die, that's about it.' But while the cameramen are plunged into and live almost inside the action, the sound man spies from across a divide. He watches but he also hears subtext and content. Sean Bean is, in Alistair's word 'magnetic'.

Forget gapping, forget even getting the takes right. When all the rubbish takes are cut out and the best is on film, Bean will be mesmerizing. When he finishes one scene, the Indian extras who must be fed up by now, can't help but burst into spontaneous applause. This is Sean's scene – Toby, for all his talent, plays to him as a foil. There's an edge of blood and death about Sean. His face is hard, alive: he's a ferret as an actor, every muscle and instinct tuned to survival.

Daragh's tale of Marlon Brando's acting lesson comes to mind. Alistair, for instance, admires Debra Winger, with whom he worked on *Shadowlands*, for exactly the reasons that Brando didn't – because, like Toby, she was utterly professional. Tea cup going down onto a saucer? Always placed exactly the same way and with consideration lest it clatter into the mike. Complicated bit of dialogue? Always delivered as agreed beforehand. Brando hated the very predictability of it all and dismissed her but not nearly with the disdain he reserved for classic English actors.

'They don't *think*. They're not actors, they're parrots. They play every scene to the back seats of the fucking theatre. The problem is, Daragh, the camera reads minds. The motion picture camera is a fucking mind reader.'

It's in Sean's eyes; it's a cunning intelligence in them which ducks constantly under danger, playing always under words. In this setting, he's punching way above his weight. If the camera is reading his mind, it'll recognize that Sean has a visceral feeling for the Sharpe character, raised from the gutter, full of resentment and flawed honour. His words aren't put in place (let alone always remembered) but seem to be dragged from him, spontaneously and from some deep place. No coincidence that his voice is dark and Toby's much stronger, more strident – in volume but more importantly, in colour. I'm reminded now of Michael Billington's regretful review of Toby's *Hamlet* that he acted 'frequently on top of, rather than through, the lines and misses the character's analytic power.' No one will make that criticism of Sean, not on film, not in this his own part. 'It's magnetism,' Alistair gives up. 'I don't know what it is. If we knew, we could train people to do it.'

Filming is full of control freaks. Even now, Katherine from costume is back in the catering tent having snatched the frying pan from the cook and is tossing her own omelette again. It's a metaphor for the longing to control every detail as a way of turning her back on filming's absurd chaos. At the same time, every man and woman on this crew longs to be carried away. And Sean has blown them off script today. He knows it too – suddenly, he's dashing, handsome, generous with his smiles, looks people in the eye, a rarity for him at the best of times, but especially on set.

When filming is going badly, you can cut the tension with a knife. Voices are clipped with unnatural politeness. As this afternoon wears on, each call from Tom Clegg of 'cut' is greeted with an immediate burst of chatter and laughter. Everyone is up. There's an atmosphere of celebration. Terry O'Neill of Aon Insurance in London can rest easy. No claim will need to be made for Sean's sickness. Almost every scene has been covered. *Sharpe's Challenge* is up to speed, or as near as matters.

At the end of this, the first week of shooting, it's averaging between 4 to 7 pages a day. Keep it up and, barring disasters, the film will finish on time and on budget. Looking on the bright side, the high maintenance Mrs Rushdie has been put safely onto a plane, and Malcolm managed to take her both to the dentist and on a cancer ward walkabout, tailed by the adoring Indian press. 'It was like being with Princess Di,' reports Malcolm. Even better, the British lines have been built in the forest and the false fort wall is nearly ready.

Tomorrow is the one day off after a long, hard six-day week. Tonight the general manager of the Trident-Hilton is hosting a poolside dinner for the entire film unit. He can't possibly understand what he has offered to do. Tonight, he has promised in a fit of enthusiasm and Indian generosity, that drinks will be free.

LEFT: *Malcolm Craddock and Tom Clegg keep talking*

BELOW RIGHT: *Julia Stannard, co-producer, takes a meeting*

BELOW: *At Diggi House; Garth, Tony and the Russian stuntmen – at the start of the night off*

TAKE 9

The Crew Parties

Mr Sudhanshu Bhushan, general manager of the Trident-Hilton over-looking the palace in the lake, must think he is about to host a corporate get-together instead of a film crew knees-up. He is spruced up in an executive dark suit and tie, greeting everyone with a fixed, bright smile. Of the £201,000 *Sharpe's Challenge* is spending on hotel accommodation (a victim of various mishaps since it was originally projected at £123,000), the Trident-Hilton is seeing the largest bite. This stylish soirée is charm personified: supper tables have been set up elegantly around the floodlit swimming pool. There's a lavish bar at one end, a buffet under burnished copper tureens at the other. A fireeater trysts with danger in one corner, next to musicians with pulsing drum and sitar. A woman dances nearby with a series of traditional water pots on her head. Very theme India, very Conde Nast Traveller, very enticing.

The film is on schedule. No one knows exactly what that means in terms of script, but it means that after the first week's shooting, the producer is happy. Malcolm Craddock is clearly so high on today's swordfight and such a self-controlled control freak himself, that he misses the threat implied by the massed bottles of spirits, wine and beer on the bar. Perhaps he doesn't miss it – heavy drinking is 'boys' stuff' to him, in the same way that *Sharpe* is 'boys' stuff'. It's what boys do. No matter that, these boys are men. 'That's actors,' he says with an almost benign pride. 'That's what they're like.'

A little background, perhaps, by way of both explanation and excuse.

OPPOSITE: *Sharpe and Harper taken prisoner by French troops working for the rebels*

First, the television unit's ethos was formed years ago when women weren't part of it – this really was men's stuff then. Maybe there was the occasional female hairdresser, but otherwise women would have almost certainly been actors or secretaries in the days when there were such creatures. Film crews take pride in the way they are and have always been cliquey riff-raff who stick together. Long shoots away from home are also new. It's only in the last few years that it's become cheaper to shoot abroad in places such as Turkey, Eastern Europe or India than in the studio back home. This intense, extended life together is a reasonably new phenomenon in TV terms.

More specifically, here in India, the evening before the day off on Wednesday is the one time the unit can unwind. Even in the Rajasthan winter, the overhead sun is merciless. It demands a strong constitution to toil in it and, besides, most people have already gone down with at least one episode of something nasty. On a Tuesday, there are two nights' sleep between the first 70-hour week and the next. Adrenalin has been flowing and the crew has lived on the swing between fear and euphoria – except, in this case, for the rigger who's getting by on boredom, but that's another story. There are age, gender and nationality fault lines running through this crew. More than ever, tonight will point up the split between Brits and Indians, the latter of whom soon sit down together at the round dining tables. The dangerous split for now is the generational one hugging the bar.

Each head of department is a small king to his team, some of which are, of course, smaller than others. Alistair Crocker, the production sound mixer, for instance, only has his loyal young acolyte, James Harbour, who's been darting tirelessly around Sean, Toby, Tom and Nigel all day with the long boom microphone. No use trying to put radio mikes on swordfighters, even if you are a sweet-faced, teetotal 25-year old with perfect teeth who has the distinction of having put his hands down Demi Moore's bra. At the beginning of a picture with a Name, crew are warned that they mustn't make eye contact, let alone touch. Demi Moore accommodated James' tender fingers without any fuss as he fixed her radio mike. He's that kind of well-meaning young man. James started off as Alistair's trainee, so the two of them work contentedly together and function as a quiet, self-contained island of sanity. Tony and Garth of Special Effects also hang together. In their case, danger isolates them and history binds them.

Director of Photography, Nigel Willoughby, on the other hand, who's washed up beautifully in his crisp hotel-laundered best, must have six on his team, four with bodies from *Men's Health* magazine, but including two extremely perky young women who load film, operate clapper boards and tout heavy cases. Since they have to function together with the rhythm of a Chinese dragon, Nigel's crew members close ranks against outsiders, protectively clustered around their leader. Whereas Marella defends Tori and Marc from all comers (no way will she allow crew to lean on Tori for free haircuts, for example), Team Nigel tends to look out for their wounded mystic.

If the telly world at home is in the hands of 30-somethings, it's experience which counts in independent television drama, where speed and shortcuts are everything. So here it's about men, it's mostly about older men and it's all about egos. Perhaps this explains why almost all the women are single; in this peripatetic life, who will they meet? On *Sharpe's Challenge*, of the women only Claire the costume designer is married. Women seem to manage by holding their ground as honorary blokes. Cry and be damned. Even though they're spiffed up for tonight, it's seems only for their own benefit – a reassurance for themselves that they exist in some way outside function.

There's a lot of female chat about shopping, mostly concerning beaded shoes and pashminas. An emergency standby costume assistant, Heidi Miller, arrived today from London. I have to suppose that she's been flown out to stem the blood-flow in the wardrobe department. Having left on a day's notice, she hasn't had time to think out the implications of role-playing and appears in a dashing dress but clinging and low-cut. Marella's cleavage is good-hearted; Heidi's is taken by the blokes to be of another kind; in crew parlance it's known as 'putting it about a bit'. Tom Clegg pounces on her with touching delight.

Mostly, for whatever reason, crews tend not to mess with one another in these early days, or at least openly, and that pretty much leaves only alcohol and foreigners. It explains the affairs, broken marriages and remarriages which came out of the early *Sharpe* films in Russia and Turkey: frustrated men meeting passionate women in the throes of an unfamiliar political freedom and free-market insecurity. That the Indians keep to themselves, especially the women, leaves alcohol as the first line of defence against stress in the Trident-Hilton.

Daragh, in stretch black T-shirt and black trousers, is a handsome blackguard wannabe but, in reality, more of a floppy and friendly Labrador retriever. Sean is the surprise: spruced up, hair washed and flying, eyes focused, smiling and enthusiastic. At 8 o'clock in the evening, he's on his best behaviour, talking of how much he's enjoying himself and how he's hoping to see something of Jaipur tomorrow. So there's the lull of false security and when the first fully-dressed crew members hit the water at 10.30, no one thinks too much about it. Certainly, no one considers the sensitivies of the Indian hosts who are fastidious about hygiene and cleanliness. Most Indians wouldn't dream of wearing shoes in their own homes, let alone in a hotel swimming pool.

Even so, when Tom Clegg gets tossed in along with the chair he was clinging to, a few wary, embarrassed souls melt away for an early night. Unfortunately, they tend to be the very people who might otherwise have sympathized with Julia's distress at being tossed in with her £400 Mark Jacob handbag holding her wallet, money, and both her UK and Indian mobile phones. Chucking in young Kate the camera loader is obviously the blokes' demonstration of affection. Different business chucking in Julia Stannard, co-producer and Gwynneth Paltrow look-alike, who negotiated everyone's contract, set the per diem at a lowly £75 a week and watches pennies to the point of complaining about people who go back for seconds in the catering tent. If watching the budget is about cutting fat to the bone, this Tuesday night off is about excess.

It's 10 o'clock on Wednesday morning. A dozen or so unit members wait for a minibus on the Trident-Hilton steps. Julia is pale, quiet and still obviously distressed following last night's 'assault'. The group is off on a long-planned excursion to join the throng at the Pushkar camel festival, three hours' drive away. Meanwhile, a car stands by for Malcolm Craddock, Tom Clegg, Michael Mallinson, Alex Sutherland and Tom McCullagh. The

Maharajah's son-in-law has reneged on the deal to rent to *Sharpe's Challenge* a few rooms in the City Palace. The pushy Bollywood producer who came up with a better offer refuses even to negotiate about sharing the space. So, at present, there are no locations in which to film Celia's bedroom, Madhuvanthi's bedroom or Wellington's library. A long day's hunt in the desert for other palaces is ahead, which for poor, tall, large Michael, the Christopher Robin first assistant director, means being crunched up for hours in the back of a van on his one day off. Thus, just when they're needed, the entire senior production team goes out of town.

Whatever the official report later and despite Malcolm's legalistic defence that no one has 'proof of what actually happened', the rumour mill wasn't in the least bit vague about what happened in the middle of last night. Leading lady Lucy Brown woke up in the lift with Sean who seemed to think he was putting her to bed. Two hours later she was back downstairs at his side and they've been drinking in the bar ever since along with Daragh, Peter-Hugo Daly, the newly-arrived supporting villain, and Caroline the continuity girl. Caroline lost one arm under a London Transport bus when she was four years old. She didn't bring her best false arm to India but she's pleased she still had her plastic one when she woke up this morning after her bender.

Daragh tells me he remembers going to bed at 5.00 for two hours. Sean, he says, hasn't been to bed at all. The dashing, handsome star has disappeared into a mean, grey wash, eyes dulled. But even in this state, he can draw people in. If he's an emotional black hole for those who should know better, it isn't entirely his fault. It isn't personal with him. Is it ever? It was one of Rajput Ram Pratap Singh's small jokes that he assigned Sean a polo pony called Sadhu. It means The Hermit. In Singh's reading of the actor, Sean doesn't connect.

Daragh wants to show everyone the enamel badge for Sheffield United football team that Sean gave him last night. He's carrying on as if it's a fraternity pledge, a token of lifelong friendship. 'Soon as he's sober, he'll take it back,' predicts a more knowing *Sharpe* veteran. The buttermilk-soft, dark-eyed and eager starlet, Lucy, is clearly in Bean thrall. She looks tired and dishevelled but game to set off to another watering hole somewhere in Jaipur, once a driver can be found.

'We don't treat actors as deferentially as they do in America,' Ben Burt, the second assistant director had boasted only last week. 'We don't mind saying "stop behaving like an asshole and get your ass on set". If you don't, there's an unbalance. It's a question of discipline and the wrong motivation. You can't have actors running things.' Empty words when it comes to the push. In the same way that no one will tell Daragh to stop feeding the monkeys, no one would dream of holding Sean to any of the rules, written or otherwise, which govern everyone else. So even Mother Courage Marella, now sitting opposite him, wondering how the hell she'll redeem his face tomorrow if he doesn't get some sleep, wouldn't dream of pulling him up, let alone holding him back.

This isn't only about Sean on set. There are some things India doesn't tolerate. Gerard the horse master has discovered, for instance, that taking explosives onto an airplane is one of them. His case is even now going painfully slowly through the legal system in Udaipur, while Sting and his wife run a distraught 'free Gerard' phone campaign from London and DOP Nigel talks about resigning on a question of principle because 'production didn't do enough for him'. And, yes, it was indeed Nigel who chucked Julia into the pool last night and is now considering a letter of apology. In the event, it becomes an offering of a pashmina, and no letter.

No one who knows believes Gerard will get off – ignorance is no plea in law. 'Oh, I didn't check my briefcase for bullets.' No defence at all. At worst it'll be a question of how long he'll spend in prison, but more likely how much it will cost. No one here can get their minds around the seriousness of the situation. Such things only happen in movies. But in a country and a city which have a history of flaring up into sudden civil disorder, riots and massacres, drinking in the streets is a similar anathema. The question is why, when Sean is in the bar the worse for drink at ten o'clock in the morning, the entire production ruling elite has gone off without leaving so much as one duty guard behind?

To understand that is to understand the paradox of film making. It's supposed to be about grown-ups but treats its stars like spoiled children. It's even supposed at times to be about reality, dealing with real problems and finding solutions – whether blowing up a cannon for action entertainment (next week, hopefully) or revisiting the anti-abortion laws (*Vera Drake*). And yet the set runs as if the rest of the world doesn't exist.

On the hill opposite Jaigarh Fort and in full view is a state-of-the-art Indian military early-warning station to monitor Pakistani planes. Seven hundred miles of Rajasthan runs along the India–Pakistan border. Hindu-Muslim conflict is never out of the newspapers, and the state is run by a Hindu Nationalist party. And yet *Sharpe's Challenge* can bring in Salman Rushdie's wife, and be surprised when local politicians with an ear to the street suggest they should be careful about her security. Whatever 'exhaustive enquiries' were made two months ago about her safety mean nothing in this volatile country. The glorious outburst of Diwali has passed; the realities of poverty and resentment have returned to Jaipur. To boot, into this cauldron, they're bringing from London the Muslim actor Alyy Khan to play Lt Mohan Singh, the one Hindu warrior hero in the film. A tentative suggestion that maybe it's a tad insensitive is met with indignant scorn. 'I believe in hiring the best actor for the job,' says Malcolm, all 'art for art's' sake' virtue.

Even now, most of the crew can't understand that Gerard can't get out of jail. They're neither hardhearted nor naive, just more blinkered than the horses Gerard couldn't produce. Softies like Nigel might resent the way the production department has distanced itself from Gerard's predicament, but he doesn't recognize the threat an association with him could pose to the project if things go badly in court. Similarly, no one treats Sean's drinking bout on a day off as a real danger – even to the actor himself, apart from anything else. It's only a question of how he'll look on set at 7.00 tomorrow morning.

In the cool late afternoon sun, a glum Malcolm finds Sean, out to the world on a sun bed by the swimming pool, side by side with Lucy, bundled in her pashmina. On the ground, lies Daragh O'Malley, a large, loving puppy guarding his master in his sleep. 'I'm not judgmental,' the producer braves it out. 'At Sean's age, I remember crawling home and my first wife refusing to let me in. My five-year-old son came down worried about Daddy and opened the door. This is *Sharpe*.'

TAKE 10

Explosions and the Clash of Cultures

There are 41 shooting days, 3 major battles, 7 skirmishes and 5 major fight sequences for *Sharpe's Challenge*. 'People say feature films are difficult. All that rehearsal time and all that money, what's difficult? Try doing it for television with no rehearsal time and not enough money,' grumbles Gareth. The stunt co-ordinator has a new headache: they are two weeks into shooting and the seven Russian stuntmen don't want to fall to their deaths for less than $500 from a horse and $700 from a tall wall. It isn't clear whether they mean one ex gratia payment or that's the fee per death. There are only seven stuntmen for the moment because one has had to be sent home with hepatitis, and his replacement hasn't yet arrived. Dr Pankaj Pandya's extempore medical tent is stuffed with the sick these days.

In the nine years since *Sharpe's Waterloo*, the Russians have become something of a star team. They earn real money at home, and are no longer the riotous, game-for-anything ingénues from the Crimea. They are wily and worldlier. I have slowly got to know them. When the Trident-Hilton asked me to leave the day before Diwali, the Rajput took me in at Diggi House. In the huge 18th-century palace, there's time with the Russians in the garden surrounded by tall trees or in the silent courtyard tucked behind the small office of Mr Wilson, the conscientious hotel manager. They may earn $1,000 even $2000 a week now, but the Russians grew up in other times, they've lived through the bleak decade after the collapse of the Soviet Union. What they know, what they've seen, separates them from the sheltered world of the grumbling Brits. When they drink – and they do – it's quiet and deadly.

They've learned to guard themselves. They certainly don't fancy cushioning their falls on the boxes which Gareth ordered by the hundred from a cardboard-making factory, somewhat unfortunately placed next to the log-chopping yard for the city's open-air crematoria. The Russians saw *Sharpe* through the years of cholera, parasites, Mafia, water shortages, low rations and food riots. They fell off horses, jumped off high walls, plunged into ravines and, for Malcolm Craddock, function as treasured mascots from the bygone glory years of early *Sharpe*, remembered as all the more golden and carefree for the years between. 'Bloody death trap,' mutters Daragh, who perhaps remembers it more clearly.

It's why, no matter what happens nor what threatens the filming in Jaipur, Malcolm can't take it seriously. 'We've known worse,' is his mantra. 'I know it sounds a bit corny to say, but we've known worse.' Although even he probably had a bad moment when Tony and Garth of Special Effects finally got to blow up a cannon. The explosion was so forceful that a wooden and iron wheel shot into the air, flew across the set and narrowly missed Nigel. The DOP might not have flinched but it hasn't improved his temper. This was when the shaken Tony came to terms with his local supplies. 'Black powder – no two bags the same. How can we guarantee anything?'

Relentless testing is one answer. The other is more interesting. Tony is coping with Indian assistants who couldn't be much use to him if they wanted to. Western and Indian SFX are worlds apart. The Indians have no idea why the bags of black powder need to be numbered and separated, why they must never be mixed. How would they know about the peril of flash powder in the mix? Why wouldn't they dole out black powder by eye and with a spoon instead of taking the time to weigh it on the precise set of scales from England? Weren't they always being rushed along anyway? The flying wheel will haunt Tony, but it won't happen again.

Instead of using his young men to fetch and carry, to perform small tasks on order and under his eagle eye, he's made some kind of personal leap and committed himself to training them. This might not sound like rocket science (forgive the pun) but there are departments where Indian assistants come in, can't immediately do the job and are sacked the same day. Before the cannon episode, Tony's men were a hurdle to get over, another bit of his problems. To him now, they're individuals.

For a start, he's learned their names. I'm taken aback by how few people around the set bother. Tony is humbled to find out that Bharat lives in a single room the size of the SFX tent with his mother, father, sister, brother-in-law and their two children. Although it isn't easy – there are barriers of language, culture and a question of trust on both sides – Tony is another of those school 'failures', and he knows what it is not to understand. This makes him a wonderful teacher. He's patient and uses humour. He's already taught them to make bullet hits. Next up, rockets. Working together, both they and he change. India has touched him, and I'm moved.

It is day 10 of filming, a quarter way through the shoot and many of the crew are reduced to monosyllabic grunts. At least, with a bit of jiggery-pokery by Mike Mallinson with the schedule, shooting is on target. Today, filming starts at 2.00 and goes on until 1.00 in the morning. It's called a 'split day', which means there is no day, only long hours in the heat and longer ones in the cold woods on the Aravalli Hills. Tomorrow, it's on to night shoots proper: nine 'days' of filming from 6.30 pm until 5.30 in the morning. At least, after a few hours in bed, it'll leave time for lunch and lazing by the pool. Even so, on such a day as this, everyone's on a short string and only the actors seem fresh and cheery.

There's a notice in the *Sharpe* production office which reads: 'It's the way we've always done it.' Some of the Brits, like Tony, are working in India with new eyes; they move along its strengths and around its problems. Tom McCullagh's art department, for example, understands that India isn't full of Georgian buildings and English period furniture, and accepts that recreating the Duke of Wellington's library will mean at best fudging, probably building from scratch and making sure a suitable desk set flies out from London with the next supporting actor. Meanwhile, Barbara and Sunil have gone off together to shop in Delhi, full of hope. For them, it's an adventure shared and the art department is working in an enchanted India.

Then there's the other approach. 'India doesn't understand how we do things, won't adapt, so we'll work in spite of it.' It ignores the country, tries to pretend it isn't there except as a backdrop and, disconcertingly, ignores most of the experienced Indian crew who know their craft but are left standing around, and are then slagged off behind their backs for the way they stand around. Considering the number of films being shipped abroad – Bulgaria, Romania, Argentina, Turkey, Toronto, anywhere that's cheaper than Shepperton or Los Angeles – it's surprising that making softer cultural landings doesn't seem to be given any kind of priority,

The *Sharpe* set, for example, doesn't take Hindi for granted, so rarely are instructions in English automatically relayed in the language spoken by most of the people on set who consequently get in the way. Since they don't expect to be included, they don't listen. Only when things go wrong are instructions belted out in Hindi and then in a fit of panic or irritation. It isn't that all the Brits are insensitive; it's the result of working in an industry in which impatience is a virtue and in a country in which the opposite is true. It isn't that the Indians are unhelpful, but Bollywood works to different rhythms and no one has probably had the time to explain the differences.

The unflappable Henry Alistair Nicholas Crocker is the victim of one such cultural misunderstanding. He sits out of the way, perched on a silver equipment box at his purpose-made Cooper Sound mixing desk, flown in from America where it was specially designed by Mr Cooper to offer ruggedness in all conditions – and wants to tear out his salt-and-pepper beard as revving Jeeps, honking horns and shouting drivers disrupt the tense 1817 encounter in the woods.

Most of the day, the unit's car drivers doze fitfully under a tree by the camels. Suddenly, the unit will be on the move, craziness sets in as cars rev to and from the filming, the drivers sitting on the horn most of the way. This would be no problem for a Bollywood shoot because sound and dialogue are recorded later and laid onto the film track in post-production. Americans and Brits work with original sound separate from, but carefully synchronized with, the camera. It's a matter of the production sound-mixer's pride that no dialogue should need to be looped or dubbed on afterwards. It's not Alistair's problem that Mrs Rushdie lets slip an occasional syllable reminding him more of New York than Jaipur, let alone that the young Princess's English is almost unintelligible. Even recording on separate tracks, background noise here has an intrusive life of its own. Jeeps roar up to the edge of the location and a cacophony of horns greet each arrival because parking is haphazard and a mess.

In any map of the film unit, Alistair would probably be the Isle of Wight, terribly English, often overlooked and crucial to defence. In the inner circle round the director, sound has no part. Tom paces and bounces, ever the elf, refusing to sit down in case anyone else follows suit. DOP Nigel has become a stalking tiger with his cubs around him. Tom the production designer is part of Tom the director's care package so tries to be on set as often as possible, while Mike the first assistant director is a pillar of reassurance in his bushwhacker's hat, fishing boots and jodhpurs. Clapper boards go, James dances around with his boom microphone desperately trying to keep it high over actors, horses and cameramen on boxes. And no one ever includes Alistair, the rock, the island. Actually, he puts it differently: 'We're the mushrooms. We're kept in the dark, and every now and again someone opens the door and throws shit all over us.'

Alistair was born into a very English social fabric. No surprise that of all his years recording top-line television, his favourite was doing *Jeeves & Wooster*. His great uncle was Sir Compton McKenzie of *Monarch of the Glen* and *Whisky Galore*, his great aunt was actress Fay Compton, his father was head of the famed BBC Natural History unit, his mother a radio producer who sat down for lunch with George Orwell, HG Wells and so on. The word 'sound' fits Alistair in every respect.

When he went to train with a film company in Bristol, it wasn't coincidence that he specialized in it. He's the sort of engineer who switched late to digital recording – not until 1997 – because he needed to count on the *reliability* of the analogue system. He had to be sure. 'Couldn't do it till we could trust it. No use coming over here and getting dust and dirt and finding no sound.' *Mrs Brown* was his last film on analogue and that was because of the wind, rain and hiking involved over the Scottish Highlands. For him, digital delivers a refinement – a difference in the dynamic range of recording between loud and soft. Now it is possible to record sound from shout to whisper and capture both. It's why a film actor such as Sean can mumble, bumble and fluff and know that the soundman will, in the end, capture the best of him.

Alistair has imagination, there's a streak of whimsy through him. He wouldn't be as good as he is, if he was only reliable. His discovery of James, for instance, whom he picked from a letter of application mentioning that he was a specialist in hip-hop. At the time, Alistair was working on a film about an animatropic rabbit. 'It's a sign, I said, a sign – we've got to have this guy.' It takes a while to make the connection, during which time he gives one of his hurrumphing chuckles. 'Right from the start, you'd say to James "run over there" and next thing you knew, he'd run 5 miles.' Eagerness and enterprise, that's what counts in the film world.

India doesn't faze the sound team but even Alistair starts to lose his impeccable control when, because of cars revving and honking, he can't record Michael Cochrane as Gen Sir Henry Simmerson shouting at top volume. To understand the impact of what happens next, you have to know the tone of insider jokes about the sound department. For example:

Question: How do you know when the soundman's dead?

Answer: When the doughnut falls out of his hand.

Alistair sets his headphones purposefully on the desk, adjusts the plastic cover over the equipment and strides up to the camera. 'It simply won't do. It will not do,' he announces at the end of his tether. Everyone in the inner circle is so surprised to see him, that action is taken immediately and cars fall silent up on the road. For a while, anyway.

Transport underpins a film set as it does a war. (Historians still debate the part played by the Russian railway timetable in the outbreak of WW1. A digression but it makes the point.) The saintly transport manager, Chand Bhatt, has to pick up actors and crew from hotels scattered around grid-locked Jaipur, miles down the hill from Jaigarh Fort. He has to find trucks to bring in tents, chairs and catering equipment to feed 500 twice a day while actors of a certain stature have to have a car of their own and a trailer of their own, and must never be asked to share. It's a sign of how jolly and on top of life Sean Bean feels that as his assigned Jeep bumps along the rocky road cut through the woods, he stops to pick up stragglers. By the time he gets back to the Fort, there are Indians and Brits hanging from all sides while Sean is crunched in the middle, and beaming.

The problem is that driving in Jaipur is a camel race with noise. Cars even drive into oncoming traffic on the wrong side of the new super-highway to Delhi. Overtaking at blind bends is obligatory. Cows, goats and dogs feed, old men, veiled women and children wander and chat as if cars aren't there – any road is both promenade and racetrack, and every driver sits on the horn. It's not for Chand from New Delhi to blast drivers hired from Jaipur: it's not the Indian way. But instead of gathering all Chand's drivers together and, through an interpreter, explaining why they need to kill engines and horns anywhere near the location, there's a short-tempered tendency to yell more loudly in English when it gets too awful. Just another culture clash.

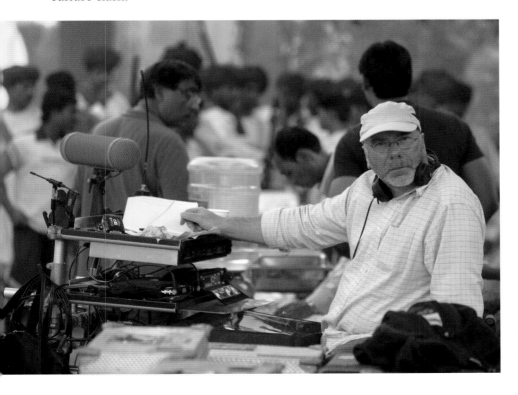

Alastair Crocker,
production sound mixer,
an island of calm

A film unit abroad perches on such clashes and misunderstandings. The logistics are so overwhelming, they have to be laid down like concrete over the natural landscape. Hence filming in this protected forest – protected by no less than India's Supreme Court which has ruled that no explosives of any kind are to be used in the country's national forests. This puts it on a par with carrying explosives onto a plane. Does the unit have clearance for blowing up a cannon and shooting off rockets in the middle of the treasured Aravalli Hills? Was there a licence to cut down trees and build this path? And when does a permitted 'path' become a 'road' anyway? Who from the Forestry Commission said what to whom and who understood what was being said in the exchange is lost in time. In short, who knows? The Indians on the crew hope for the best and pray the film unit will get away with it. Most of the Brits operate in sublime unawareness.

As it happens, there won't be any rockets today, and that's another of the culture clashes. Garth Inns is so desperate by now, he's falling back on his story about filming in freezing snow in Iceland and watching with relief as the catering truck slowly worked its way up the hill, to find that it carried only one urn of tea for a crew of 80. For sure, one day, when some other special effects are giving him a hard time somewhere, he'll be telling the tale of *Sharpe* and the rockets disaster.

After the cannon imbroglio, Tony and Garth are taking no chances with the rockets. These are the ones supposedly fired from the fort on the British lines which are so frightening, they cause mayhem and panic. Three hundred of them are meant to rain down; that was the plan. Back in England, Tony was expecting to import tiny, machine-made American rocket engines to fire them off. Now he understands why he was passed round the Indian High Commission from desk to desk. Ever polite, no Indian would want to give him the bad news. Rocket engines? Out of the question.

Pyrotechnic experts were flown in from Delhi and Mumbai, all of whom promised to deliver rockets to specification. Of course, he believed them: the Indians invented rockets and, besides, Diwali lit up the Jaipur sky for days and anyone planning to set off a bomb could not have made more noise. What he has now realized to his dismay is that the rockets are obviously going to be made by hand. There are no rocket factories in India.

Right now, ingenuity and craftsmanship counts for nothing. Tony longs for the predictability and control which machines deliver. Since the Indian special effects' supervisor, Arun Patil, has already felt the cold lash of English impatience over delays and broken promises, he has taken to sitting in a chair outside the tent. Meanwhile, Tony, Garth and the newly-enthused assistants patch together some form of rocket on the bench in the SFX tent. So far, of the 300, either 12 or 20 are ready for the woods. Ten men have been fanned out around the location, each touting a mask and large water pump. The set has been cleared for a test. Tom Clegg warns everyone to watch carefully and to dive for cover if necessary. Tony hits the walkie-talkie, Garth lights the rocket. And absolutely nothing happens. Not with the first, not with the second, not ever. Suddenly no one wants to talk to Tony; it's as if India is his fault.

There is one small but touching sign of cultural sensitivity. Alex (aka Alejandro) Sutherland, production supervisor, has a Scottish father, a Spanish mother and a Turkish wife. He's learned to listen. He has rented for the unit a deserted Hindu temple which stands close to the location in the woods. The caterers lay tables inside the palatial temple hall and set up a cramped tent outside in the yard. Of course, the British crew think the inside dining hall is for the A team, which gets Western and meat dishes. In fact, they have been pushed outside and left to stand around. It's the Indian B & C teams which get to sit down with Lord Krishna. Alejandro knows better than to bring non-vegetarian food into a holy temple. Maybe he would have got away with it, but sometimes there are more important things than just 'getting away with it'.

TAKE 11

ADs – The Systems Men

*S*harpe's Challenge has no less than five assistant directors and two runners in charge of managing the set. Let me correct that: *Sharpe's Challenge* has no less than five assistant directors and two runners on the payroll. Three and a half of them manage the set. Nothing underscores the personal nature of authority and its importance to a film, particularly one which is on such a tight shooting schedule (i.e. just about all television drama) than the increasing irrelevance of the other three and a half.

Does anyone suppose authority can be taught? Certainly, it can be communicated by example but I can't imagine it an effective subject for a film school lecture. Not that many of the people running the set here have much use for film school, or even university as a requirement for anything anyone actually does. First AD, Michael Mallinson's view is typical: 'They do media studies and then confuse what we do with "The Imagery of Alfred Hitchcock. Discuss".'

This is what ADs do – or at least, what they do here, given that everything is about relationships which must change from film to film, personality to personality. Bear with me, and you'll see what this means. During the now golden age of pre-production, Mike went through the script and planned the shooting schedule, page by page, scene by scene. Hunched over his laptop in the production office, tapping away into his Movie Magic Scheduling software, he was a picture of happiness: nothing a good first AD enjoys as much as the challenge of intricate, seemingly

OPPOSITE: *Ben Burt, 2nd A.D., walks the actors*

impossible planning. This is his one moment of control – or least the illusion of it.

Mike broke down the script and compressed scenes into as tight a fit as possible: the idea being to take as few sweeps as possible at locations, or with actors, special effects, animals or stuntmen. Use them up, sweep them out, send them home. Above all, keep movement between locations to the very minimum. Pages and snippets of pages, scenes out of sync but happening on the same location, night scenes bunched together. Of course, it ends up an actor's nightmare: Sean Bean has to bid Lucy Brown's Celia a fond farewell weeks before meeting her. It's all about money. It's always about money. Picture the time and expense in taking down and putting up all those catering tents for a start. Of course, everything gets thrown into the air when Tom Clegg punches holes in the schedule as he goes along. Never mind. For a couple of weeks, Mike was happy.

Once filming started, Mike placed his two sturdy legs – always trousered, never in shorts – next to the camera and became the large, still point of the unit, running the floor while the director floated around it like an asteroid in space. When you can't pinpoint Tom Clegg's where-abouts, you can always find Mike Mallinson. His is the first-AD-as-tent-pole way of managing the set. And nothing illuminated the personal nature of his authority more than the day he went sick. It wasn't that scenes didn't get shot or mistakes were made. It's that there was a hole in the ether; a reassuring security blanket went missing.

When Mike was ill, the second AD, Ben Burt, stepped up to the plate. Ben is two decades younger, more in the dancing-Clegg mould than the stand-and-deliver Mallinson's. Frankly, many of the crew preferred Ben's enthusiasm to Mike's seen-it-all calm but that's to underestimate the importance of the tent pole in a storm. Part of Ben's different approach is a reflection of his age and his passion for football and cricket. Part is because he's used to the second AD's role, which is to act as the eyes and ears of the first AD. He's used to whizzing about the place. He has to hunt down possible problems which might not surface for a week, while constantly sorting out crises large and small, preferably before they get to the set. Wardrobe, for instance. Ben Burt has become an expert in the emotional battlefield which is the costume department. He is often to be seen restlessly roaming around trailers, buses and tents sniffing trouble before it bursts. Meanwhile, he's also making sure everyone is in the right place at the right time, every time, right now.

Ben's job is to see that everyone has transport, horses turn up, actors take riding lessons, get to costume fittings or see the doctor. He's the systems man who gets the ground ready before shooting starts: do make-up facilities make sense, is there a production line for getting actors and extras ready, will it work under pressure? He draws up the call sheet each night, re-does it when Mike has to rearrange shooting at the last moment and then makes certain everyone gets one – which in Jaipur, with crew and actors scattered over a dozen, distant hotels, is heavy duty. 'The real test of the job,' says Ben 'is if you can pay the same attention to detail at 11 o'clock at night after an 18-hour day as you do in the morning.'

For a young man who worked in Mexico on *Troy* and was in charge of dressing sets with a thousand extras, *Sharpe* isn't a 'massive job'. 'It's being pushed for time, but that's nothing new. Being a Second AD is about being in control. Anywhere you're working with crew, you're working with creative people with fraught personalities, which is why the best Seconds I know are the most poker-faced. This film can't afford to have people who demand privileged treatment. If you can still give out an air of control no matter what, it helps to calm everyone else.' Ben isn't poker-faced: it's that no matter how pinched and white he looks, however red and screwed up his eyes when he crawls into the Trident-Hilton hours later than anyone else, he doesn't make a production of it. He isn't one of the unit's martyrs – there are more than enough of those.

In theory, two British ADs might have been enough. There's a second AD (India) and a third AD (India), lovely young men who arrived in Jaipur from Mumbai and sat on chairs in the production office waiting to be given responsibility and told what to do (an oxymoron, obviously). By contrast, the day Ben Burt arrived, he found a table, opened his laptop and set to work, making the film his own. So if I point out that the Indian second assistant director has pretty much been reduced to cueing the dancing girls – no, seriously – and that the 3rd AD's job is mainly confined to holding up traffic near the location – with no great success – perhaps you can see how everything in the end boils down to confident, personal authority.

On the other hand, one of the Indian runners, KP, has emerged as an unexpected star. KP is known to all and knows everyone both by name and job. His sunny smile has lit up many a pre-dawn. He is willing, attentive and quick at anticipating ways to be useful, so Mike and Ben have started to rely on him. The test is how rarely you'll hear them call for him – he's always where he's needed – but how often are the names of the hapless Indian 2nd and 3rd Ads heard over the set or through the walkie-talkies. Everything's relationships.

It was clear from the start that Mike and Ben couldn't run Jaigarh Fort by themselves. For a start, it wasn't going to close to visitors and from the time *Sharpe's Challenge* moved in during pre-production, it has been plagued by curious onlookers – almost all of them noisy and uninhibited. The terrain is spread out and hard going, and the hundreds of extras are

Catering tent A: Mike Mallinson checks the shooting schedule; Tom McCullagh (left)

inexperienced. Behind the closed doors during The Countdown, production decided to fly out a third AD from England, to act as Mike Mallinson's legs on set.

Enter David Higgs, a handsome, full-lipped, rosy-cheeked 21-year old who was hired over the phone, flown out and chucked into a Jaipur fleapit by himself, all other hotels being strangled with tourists for Diwali. He bounced about the very next morning in a scrumptious, white linen shirt, which prompted ribald teasing from the make-up mavens. Undaunted, David span around: 'This is Hugo Boss.' 'And this,' said Marella, pinching her plump arm 'is gin.' Laughter, immediate rapport.

David marches about the set, utterly focused, tireless, and does anything that needs to be done: he calls for quiet, sends messages on the walkie-talkie, pulls extras back into place, comforts the sick, and never takes his eyes off Mike (or Tom Clegg, when he can see where the director has bobbed off). It's a virtuoso performance, rather like being the one violinist at the back of an orchestra who sits up straight and plays with confident attack. Natural authority: this is the essential quality for an AD – well, that and a supportive, well-off, middle-class family, preferably with connections in the film business.

David got his break through a family friend's brother. Ben's father is the successful producer Chris Burt who asked Mike Mallinson to hire his son as an 18-year-old runner on the early *Sharpe* films. Ben at 30 is almost the only person on *Sharpe's Challenge* who has Sean Bean's private mobile number – as high a measure of success as it's possible to get.

All three effective assistant directors on this shoot learned by experience, and two of them started at the bottom. Mike Mallinson is the exception. He is also the only one of the three to be in constant work, and that, he says, is because he's old (55) and the equivalent of an experienced sergeant major. This is putting himself down, since he's not there simply to carry out orders and boss about the troops: he's there to shape the way the film is shot, to pre-empt, not to follow. But putting himself down is Mike's way. It is the defence of bungled dreams. His ample voice was honed at the Central School and LAMDA. Acting? 'Oh, I was sadly lacking in talent. I was always going to be an also-ran.'

Instead he went into theatre production and ended up managing the Young Vic until a friend pointed him towards Thames Television drama department. There followed years of running weekly drama productions with major actors such as Celia Johnson and Paul Scofield. 'It was the golden age of television, when, in a sense, you didn't have budgets.' (How often do I hear that elegy for the past?) In the same way that television sent him on courses and trained him to find locations, do deals, manage the floor, supervise the filming, he could have stepped up to direct. Those were the days when television companies nurtured their talent. 'If you want to be a director, you have to have a passion to do it. I think directors and actors are similar in that way – it's as if it's *got* to happen. I never felt that.'

Instead, he settled for this life as first AD, the man who controls the people who make the film. 'Youngsters, they all turn round and say, "I want to be a producer, a director, a DOP or sound" – no one says what I really want to be is an AD. I'm sure there's no course for it, let alone a text book, nothing that explains what we do – well, I've never managed to explain what I do to my mum.'

His image on set is that of the reliable, solid Head Boy but he's a more reflective, sadder, figure in private. There are chequered shadows across his life as there are to most of the men here: a 19-year-old son by neither his first nor even his Portuguese second wife – he met the latter in the Crimea as a hairdresser on the first *Sharpe*. The shadows were probably always there and showed in the way he immediately responded to the one-off nature of television drama compared to the job he turned down managing the Royal Court Theatre. 'To be honest, I was sort of bored with the theatre. I whizzed off into the TV business thinking the grass was greener …' Yes, there are now two homes in Portugal, the café he and his wife are renovating – but he almost always has to work away from his adopted home. 'In my time, I've worked on a lot of car run-bys in the Acton High Road.'

Ben Burt's first job as a runner for Mike was more glamorous: a stint in Russia on *Sharpe*, as a compromise instead of a gap year in India and Thailand and a Film Studies place at a not very distinguished university. He's yet another of those bright men on this unit who dreamed away his schooldays: 2 Cs and a B at 'A' level doesn't do much credit to Latymer School. Plunging into life as a floor runner, the job set him free: he worked long hours, ran messages, did the photocopying, took mail to the post office and learned to assess priorities. 'You can't have scripts delayed because you're getting the dry cleaning for the producer but then, if you've got an important producer, it may be the dry cleaning has priority. You learn.'

He learned to fetch endless teas, coffees and breakfasts for needy actors. 'Everyone undervalues that. It's important that they don't turn around at 8 o'clock when shooting has started and say, "Got to go and have my breakfast."' He walked actors from their car to the trailer, reassured and nurtured them and quickly realized that if a runner's any good, actors won't be difficult. Ben did that for about three years, working 14 hours a day, earning anything between £70 and £400 a week. It's his view, having exploited more than a few runners himself since then, that 'floor running makes or breaks.'

From left: Dave the Best Boy,
John the Grip, Tom the Gaffer

From the start Ben has been part of Mike's team. It doesn't mean they always work together, or even often. Mike's pre-production weeks mean he's often out of sync with his chosen 2nds and 3rds by the time he's in a position to hire them. It's how young David Higgs got here. By the time the production department was ready to hire someone from England, none of Mike's usual 3rd ADs could come on a day's notice. So Mike phoned someone he trusted who recommended David. In the business, it's always who you know.

In present working conditions – or lack of them – men with rent and mortgages have to take the jobs they can get. Ben nearly didn't make it to India: he was offered three weeks on a Ridley Scott big-budget film. A tough decision: anything with Ridley Scott would be more prestigious than 10 weeks on *Sharpe*: 'But if I'd done that, I would have been at home doing nothing for six weeks and I'd be brain dead. Besides, it's incredibly expensive to be in London without working because you have to get out, see friends and stay involved – that's how you hear what films are going on.'

There are 2nd ADs who don't want to move up and on, the most famous being Michael Stevenson, who was honoured at BAFTA with the Balcon Award – basically for being the actors' best friend. It's the 2nd AD who gets the chat in the trailer, the bonding on the walks to the set, the lavish presents and hugs from Names at the end of a shoot, the thanks for arranging trips with the wife. Or not the wife. Much more glamorous, perhaps, than calling: 'Quiet for rehearsal, please'. But Ben, another of *Sharpe*'s clever, organized control freaks with a messy family life can't wait to be 1st AD.

That's the sum of his ambition: not to produce like his father, nor to direct, but to be the infallible retainer. The problem is that any feature film with over a £1.5 million budget has to be bonded – a form of insurance that if the film goes over budget, the bond company will pay to complete it. A bond company, however, is cautious: it will, for example, demand to vet the crew list and wouldn't take a chance on a first-time 1st AD. So for the time being, Ben Burt is happy to bide his time and wait for a break in television. 'It's a hard living. It's a 6-day week and you don't get a lot of money. Problem is, I've never been able to work out what else I'd do. This is the only thing I've ever worked at or wanted in my life.'

Not totally honest, of course. Any AD worth his salt would rather work 18 hours a day on a big-budget feature. It's why Mike Mallinson gets a certain pinched pleasure from the fact that the snobs from feature films seem to have got their come-uppance: 'There are almost no feature films being made in the UK now so there's no work – television people have won out. But it's all about which circuits you're on and what you're being paid. If I was doing this on a feature film, I'd be earning at least £3,000 a week and in television these days, I'd be lucky to earn £50,000 a year. But on big-budget films you get paid for the politics. Look at the first three pages of a unit sheet for any feature film and it's all executives before you get to anyone who turns over. Politics are *much* trickier. I'm just one of the oiks. Look around: we're all oiks here.'

He says that, but he also says, 'If you're any good at the job, you should be able to stand on the set and foreigners should know immediately who's in charge.' By 'foreigners', he means civilians, outsiders. One day an unfortunate extra forgets to turn off his mobile phone and Bach's *Toccata and Fugue* rings out over Jaigarh Fort. Immediately, all eyes, unit, kibbitzers and tourists alike, turn not to the culprit but to Mike Mallinson. One stern flash of an eye – and no mobile phone interrupts a shot again.

TAKE 12

Battle Stations

Ben Burt reads books about mountaineering and regards *Into Thin Air* as 'one of the greatest books I've ever read'. He doesn't climb so for him it is both metaphor and a triumph of imagination over reality. I should have paid closer attention to his choice.

To anyone who associates film-making with the overblown silkiness of Hollywood, the crowd scene in the bar of the Trident-Hilton of Jaipur would probably disappoint and deceive by its ordinariness. Daragh O'Malley estimates that when he and his wife lived in Los Angeles – by no means extravagantly in his starry vision of extravagance – he couldn't get by with less than $20,000 a month net, and that is renting not buying an apartment, leasing not buying a car, in a city cheaper than London. Sean Bean and Toby Stephens apart, there can't be many here earning much more than Mike Mallinson's £50,000 a year before tax. Throw in periods of work famine, mortgages, children, wives, ex-wives and pet food and it explains the crabby one-liners in Catering Tent A every Monday as the cash for per diem allowances is handed out. More to the point, it explains the black jokes and doom-saying engendered by shooting on a limited budget and working against deadlines, while knowing that ahead is the bleak month of January and probable unemployment. Like the lives of its crew, the filming of *Sharpe's Challenge* is a triumph of invention and imagination over reality.

After 10 days of filming, there is the first of 9 night shoots. The storm-

ing of the impregnable Ferraghur Fort by the British troops (for which read Jaigarh) produces an almost twisted pleasure in predicting failure and humiliation: rockets won't go off; set off explosions at the breach of the newly-built fort wall and the whole structure will topple over; the Indian extras will be too afraid to climb the precipitous approach in the dark, and if they do, they'll fall over. A few lone souls from production adopt the confidence of in-store saucepan salesmen – and convince no one. Tony Auger, the special effects co-ordinator, is noticeably ashen-faced and the veteran SFX technician, the Falstaffian Garth, has fallen silent. They chain-smoke. It is, an outsider might think, the quiet before the storm of failure.

And this is to miss the old-fashioned, WW2 doggedness of seasoned British TV stalwarts. It's as if, in putting themselves down, they reckon to creep around the ire of the gods. It is Richard Todd in *The Dam Busters*, Jack Hawkins in *The Cruel Sea*: understated men going out to do their duty against the odds. An exaggeration? Just watch Tom the director leap out night after night onto a hill which is almost vertical, and refuse to change his Desert Rat shorts for trousers or to put a sweater over his short-sleeved cotton shirt. And then watch the crew slithering down across rocks and dust to join him.

This is where the quiet, thoughtful dominance of Tom the production

The Pindaris attack: stuntmen with polo ponies from the Rajasthan Polo Club and Diggi House

designer makes itself felt. It is one thing to design a showy new fort wall for everyone to admire, another to spend untold and unseen hours going over the slope with a team of labourers, picking up every stone and rock, smoothing every patch of dust on which the soldiers will be running up (and gingerly clambering down again) and on which a large proportion of them will be dying. He has made it as easy as he can, even to the extent of putting in new stones for footholds. But what he has also done is, by using the trees which are there, built boulders into the hillside to create the look of every, brown, dusty battlefield hanging on a museum wall. At last, I truly understand what's meant by 'The Look' of the film.

The men of Forlorn Hope have to get up this cold, desert slope venting blood-curdling battle cries while remembering to skirt the explosive devices Tony has buried in the dust. This is the desert; dark is absolute. Were this being done on a feature film budget, the whole of this 'western slope' would be bathed in lights from cherrypickers. As it is, Tom Gates the gaffer with his Indian assistants has done wonders with lamps balanced on the battlements. Most of these were scrounged from a Bollywood acquaintance met in Mumbai who took Tom home to meet his wife, children and opened his lighting store to him. 'Gaffers' honour', Tom calls it, although even he's not sure it would happen in Denham or Chesham. Even so, the

hill will have to be stormed in small sections, bit by bit, puddle of light by puddle of light.

A few days ago, Tony and Garth blew a vast hole in the false fort wall aided by Bharat, Ajay and Salim: a partnership has been forged. Here is where the single-mindedness which shuts out all other worlds comes into its own. Tom McCullagh trucked in several tons of carefully chosen boulders from a local quarry and then built them up to form the ultimate cascading breach. It's action stuff with the care of flower arranging, not that it's certain anyone would have noticed had he tipped up the back of the truck and dumped the lot. The storming of the Maharajah's cliff-top fort by the British Army is a major climax of the film and undoubtedly it will be layered with stirring, heart-busting music. Will anyone really sit at home and notice Tom's hand-picked breach? Still, the devil – or virtue – is in the design and production detail. It explains why Tom himself is here all night until 5.00 in the morning, and why he roams the ramparts and skitters down the slope, restless and alert.

At 2.00 in the morning, he pounces on some unfortunate Pindari soldier in the ranks wearing a turban of vivid *lime* green. Moments before the rehearsal, Tom whisks it off and insists that wardrobe run back to find a more muted green to fit The Look. At first, he seems like a madman, carried away by fatigue. The soldier was right back in the ranks. The hillside and ramparts are by now almost impenetrable with smoke from the ghastly-smelling cow-dung patties being burned everywhere in steel dishes.

It isn't until all the red-coated British and Indian soldiers are put in place, man by man, on the hillside and the lighting casts its mysterious shadows over the invented uniforms of the Pindaris that the significance of Tom's chillingly obsessive eye becomes apparent. The hillside scene, paused and frozen awaiting command, is an oil-painting, hundreds of years old, on which the must and dust of time have muted all colour. When film-makers talk of 'collaboration', this is what they mean: the way every part of the scene folds into the other – the lighting which Tom the gaffer has created for and in Nigel's fluid vision, the way the uniforms have been powdered, aged and beaten to reflect the dust of miles of marching. The way there isn't one absolute red uniform, some more weathered, others less as, indeed, they would have been. The way that the brown earth shows through on the hill, where before clusters of white stones broke and fragmented it. And, once action is called, the way the lights play on the exploding flames and shimmer through the smoke, as up the ridiculously steep Aravalli hill pour wave after wave of young Indian men who, but a few short weeks ago, were gathered from the streets of Jodhpur and Jaipur.

None of this will count for anything if there is nothing here to make the Forlorn Hope forlorn. It all depends on the shower of rockets to be sent over the walls by Garth while Tony hides behind a tree detonating charges to suggest cannon fire and shot to cut down the oncoming British troops. If this isn't stupendous and 'real', if we as viewers feel fooled, it's going to look about as silly as a load of granddads reconstructing Waterloo on some field in Kent, or Gettysburg on some Texan meadow.

Tony's earlier rockets, victims of Indian artistry in Mumbai, Delhi and Jaipur, not to mention the high security alert, had cost £600 before he threw up his hands. He probably regrets having said at one point: 'It's not a job to me. It's the scary excitement of not knowing what's going to happen.' But not for nothing had this Biggles imported his irascible helpmate. 'Garth is very, very clever. Things I wouldn't think about, he does.' As absurd as it sounded at the time, Tony took up Garth's suggestion that they go out into the Pink City and buy ordinary rockets from a local firework store.

The Diwali light and sound show continues nightly over Jaipur, blinding and deafening us all; showers of stars and rockets still fill the skies. As a last, what-the-hell measure and for a handful of rupees, Tony and Garth bought boxes of rocket motors, came home, and with some plastic drainpipe tubing, paper cups, paper cones and black paint and the help of the now dextrous SFX team, built their own rockets. Lo and behold, a shower of the things fizz over the ramparts, scudding down onto the hillside, flaming light against black sky and, on cue, cutting straight across the two cameras wielded by Nigel and Tom, below a third operated from on high by Kate the loader. And when the pyro-fiends set off the explosion in the tunnel, and dust and burning cow-dung smoke heap onto and into everyone anywhere near, no one cares. It's a triumph. It's going to look stunning.

Gareth choreographs the fight:
Sean beats up Bickerstaff
(Peter-Hugo Daly)

It isn't that there are cheers, or even smiles. Just the casual grumbling of the Brits doing their thing against all odds and seemingly more interested in the Fray Bentos steak and kidney pies being flown in from London for Sean Bean. And when I find Tom McCullagh to say how awed I was by the sight, he brushes aside the compliment in his slow, flat voice, as he always does. Apart from the times we talk of his children, I hear his voice quicken only once: it's the day he comes across Ben Burt playing an extempore game of cricket in the car park with some young Indian boys. 'If only we'd got something like that going in Belfast ...' he says with such feeling, I can almost taste it.

This making do and lack of fuss explains why so many American blockbusters used to be made in England. And it also explains the bewilderment that a revised tax code has killed such film-making in Britain. There is no satisfaction in this cold, desert night that *Sharpe's Challenge* is a big, old-fashioned action movie being made for the small screen.

Not that the evening isn't without its lighter moments. The young men from Jodhpur, painfully thin and desperately sweet for the most part, were recruited two weeks before those from Jaipur and consider themselves to be superior as a result. Inter-city gang warfare has broken out and in the far reach of the Fort next to Catering Tent C, a real stone-throwing battle is in progress before anyone realizes and puts an end to it. Now all the Indian extras have been court-martialled onto the cobbled square by the Breach to be kept under the panicky eye of the dismal Indian second AD. His fear of insurrection is betrayed by his voice barking higher and higher up the scale as the night goes on – with less and less result. Never have I felt so vindicated about the importance of natural authority and the confidence to be polite.

Tonight, at last, John Rhymer, standby rigger, has come into his own after weeks of good-tempered boredom. If there's anything over 6ft to be put up, the rigger has to be called in to do it. Unlike most other departments where the Indian crew hang about while the Brits battle for glory, the Indian riggers have taken everything upon themselves. John is nevertheless essential because he's Health & Safety and it's up to him to watch out for everyone's safety every time anything's rigged. However, in three weeks of shooting, he hasn't done more than put up one 7ft camera tripod.

Fortunately, he is not a generic rigger which, according to the rest of the crew, is a hard-bitten, foul-mouthed, bad-tempered, hard drinker (which, coming from this crew, is something of a show-stopper). 'It's just because they're always doing something dangerous,' says John defensively. 'They have to prove how tough they are.' John, on the other hand, is a fair-haired, warm-hearted Glaswegian who whips open his wallet to show off the photograph of his beloved Llasa Apso, and has been combing the local gem market for the perfect present for his wife, and spending on her more than his entire per diem for the shoot.

Until tonight, his real contribution has been in buzzing about between the woeful, burning up his energy in spreading some of his good humour. Without the riggers, there would be no lights mounted on the highest point of the battlements. And what is heart-warming is that he takes no credit for it and directs all compliments to the Indian crew, who can be seen as dots perched way above on the Fort's narrow ledges. It is a display of craftsmen's skill on the one hand and generosity on the other.

The mesmerizing sideshow is the tussle between Tom the director and Gareth the stunt co-ordinator. Whenever something works, Tom wants more. A big bang? Great, let's have two of them. More cannon fire, more of everything. This is Tom Clegg's forte: he loves the thrill of complex action scenes. Who can blame him? At last he's free of actors' egos, actors' fallibility. He has toys to play with and an army to march. His momentum makes what's happening down there on the slope more exciting both on and off the camera, but if there's one thing a stunt co-ordinator doesn't like, it's spontaneity. This is make-believe painstakingly planned. There are real lives at stake in the black night.

Gareth's other gripe is the way Tom clings to the Russian stuntmen. These latter must touch a nostalgic nerve in Tom; they were with him through the early *Sharpe* films and the dangers of the Crimea. He prefers them over the Indian stuntmen from Mumbai whom Gareth has carefully trained to do the Indian soldiers' stunts. No, says Tom, I want the Russians. No matter that they are currently togged out as Brits and will hold up shooting while they're despatched to make-up to be blown apart as Indians, and will then have to be turned back again into Europeans to plunge 12 ft from the battlements onto Gareth's cardboard boxes at the finally agreed figure of £250 per death.

It's reasonable to suppose that English stuntmen would take half a day to rehearse this backwards somersault over the high wall. But Tom Clegg is pushing to move forward: there are no still moments, the battle marches on. The Russians know the risks. Any sensible stuntman would prefer to see the pad he's falling onto but smoke from the explosions means that no one here will see anything. Now Tony's as concerned as Gareth. Oleg, as befits a physicist from a St Petersburg research institute, spends his last minutes doing the fall 20 or 30 times in his mind and then throws himself over the wall, trusting to the memory in his body. It's a mesmerizing display of courage. Later, when it's all over, Gareth is moved to song over a clutch of Kingfishers and Tony drowns his joy in whisky, saying again and again: 'I love these guys, they're absolutely brilliant. I love them to bits.'

Much amusement is to be found in the Russians' absolute indifference to everyone else and the way that, between each death, they pitch onto the nearest patch of dust and fall fast asleep. Watching this mini-drama affords considerable distraction at first; after a while, it raises in my mind serious questions of responsibility. Each head of department has to fill in and file a safety form for each scene, warning of all possible dangers and hazards. Gareth's is the ultimate responsibility for stunts: it is up to him, as specialist, to guarantee safety. Each time Tom Clegg overrides him, Mike the first AD loyally backs up his director, sending Gareth into a sulk of worry. It's called 'flying by the seat of my pants', and tonight they get away with it spectacularly.

But there are those who remember that Daragh O'Malley had one whole side of his face kicked in by an English army hobnail boot during what was, as he remembers it, an under-rehearsed fight in pouring rain and dangerously slippery mud in the Crimea. He needed major plastic surgery to put his face together again. It's a moot question during these long, difficult hours – but one never quite resolved – as to whose safety regulations pertain to a British crew filming in anarchic India. No one I ask seems to think it matters, except Gareth. Meanwhile, they're on the other side of the world from London and tonight has been an unmitigated triumph for a dog-tired team.

During the endless night shoots, one other question keeps wriggling worm-like into my mind. For hours, I've watched Marella, Marc and Tori climb down the hill to pour blood onto extras and tie ghastly silicone wounds to their bodies. It's convincing and ghoulish. Suppose one of these young men was actually killed in a freak accident, and that take was the best. What would be the ethical argument against using it? That it would be obscene? Well, if the reality would be obscene, why is this bloodied make-believe violence less so?

It is a philosophical problem and I don't like to bring it up in the middle of the night on the top of a mountain, but I do mention it to the Rajput who has come to watch the mayhem. He turns a fierce, dismissive eye on me: his caste, he points out, was bred for hundreds of years for warfare. Aggression is in man's nature. Well, perhaps so, but preferably not. And maybe it's just a woman's response to driving through the old city's reality on the way to watching too much boys' stuff.

OPPOSITE TOP: *Ben organizes cricket*

BOTTOM: *Camel delivery truck*

ABOVE: *Breach bloody blows at last*

OPPOSITE TOP: *Indian palace background,
Muir and Toby*

RIGHT: *Tea time at the topi: the waiter is a
qualified pathologist who makes more
money from this, his day job*

TAKE 13

The Break – Time Off

There are nine days of night shoots from 6 pm to 5 am, followed by the regular day off and then a rest day. It's not that I'm tired – I'm cold, all the time. I have been here over a month, and through 19 long days of filming. The hot sun burns but doesn't warm me. My kind Diggi House Rajput hosts react with a thick cardie and a puffer heater. I go to bed in my prized Jaipur Polo Club fleece, which can't be worn to location because it's become the *Sharpe's Challenge* trophy of choice and Tom the director hasn't got one. It was given – or, rather, bestowed – by the unbending Rajput, Ram Pratap Singh, and it means much that he allows me to call him by his nickname 'Naina'. I've enticed his wife, Jyotika, to a quaint gym round the corner, and we set off together every day to Naina's great amusement as he walks his property.

I understand why the film crew bonds so quickly. Until I moved to Diggi, I felt outside of time and alone. Here, there are the Russians, all shadowy melancholy expressed in song after enough whisky, rum and Kingfishers. Gareth and Tony have taken to hanging out in this island of peace, and everyone is invited to watch Naina play polo, a strange juxtaposition of stiffly attired bagpipe bands, cavalry officers and a host of Indian tut-tut drivers scrambling onto fences to watch.

And then there's Abhijit Sen Gupta, Gareth's haughty assistant horse master from Bangalore, who functions as a Greek chorus, distant, judging, full of sudden outbursts, but able to laugh at himself and, alas, also at us.

OPPOSITE: *Moving into the desert*

His English is posher than ours, his Indian pride contained but keener than our own feeble loyalty. His is a curious independence and for some reason it doesn't bother Gareth that Abhijit doesn't turn up for work unless he considers there's something to be done. Thus the Diggi House Set breathes out during these two days off.

The extra time off is probably good for everyone: there are fractures in the firmament. Nigel Willoughby can hardly hide his impatience at the way the director pushes him aside to peer through Camera A and line up shots. Sometimes Nigel must feel as if he is Tom's lowly camera operator. There's an old joke in the business:

Question: What's the difference between God and a Director of Photography?

Answer: God doesn't think he's the DOP.

Not very funny on those night shoots at Jaigarh.

Similarly, Gareth still growls like a bad-tempered bear at the way Tom Clegg rearranged one after another of his complicated stunts. Legally, it's the stunt co-ordinator's role and responsibility to train and organize stuntmen and extras. But Tom had the battle in his head, and it wasn't quite the same as Gareth's.

Despite Gareth, the days off afford a chance to stand back, to see Tom Clegg more sympathetically. Megatons of power land on a director during shooting. This may be the producers' film but for now everything and everyone is Tom's to command. Three quarters of the time he's sitting on top of a capsized boat, but a quarter of the time he's trapped underneath it. Yes, it's an intolerable strain but power has found out his tiny character flaw and he's riding roughshod over others. It isn't that he's a monster (most directors are, I'm assured) but he can be a bully. The question is whether at the end of this, he can get his own character back and become again the man first met during the days of pre-production.

Tom is shooting scenes as narrowly as possible, cutting in his head as he goes along. This is partly because the burden of such a tight shooting schedule weighs on him. But there is something more involved. Consciously or not, Tom is going to offer up as few choices as possible to post-production. He is making sure that it's *his Sharpe's Challenge* which goes out, not some invisible editor's in London. Tom Clegg is a realist – if, at 71, this should turn out to be his swansong, he wants to be the one who sings it.

There's one person on the set who can deal openly with Tom. It isn't Malcolm – even he wraps Tom in cotton wool, grateful that at least the director talks to him. There must be times when Malcolm wields his producer's wand and puts his foot down, although I never see it, nor I suspect does anyone else. Everyone on the set comes in for niggardly criticism at some time, even the nicest of them. 'He's a lovely man,' someone says of another, 'but so *boring*.' Digs like that hurt, and are hard to forget. Daragh invites me to join a group who are off to Clark's Hotel for an outing. 'I don't want her,' Sean mutters. 'She's a spy.' That alone cuts, but what cuts more is that everyone around him nods.

The only person no one has a bad word about is Caroline O'Reilly, the script supervisor, and she's the one person who can handle Tom at his most irascible and stubborn. It's hard to catch time with Caroline. She's on set every day, all day, perched near the camera on her trademark black fold-up stool, balancing her large bundle of papers and moving both for each new set-up with her one arm. And, of course, no one helps. Even when she's horribly ill, she shows up, tottering but focused.

Caroline writes down each take and then makes a note for the editor back in London whether or not there was sync sound and, more important, why the take went wrong, or what Tom was looking for and which take was best, or at least the director's choice. Meanwhile, she's watching out for continuity. There's a row over whether the ensign was or wasn't wearing a hat in a previous shot during the approach to the breach. Tom is resolute: no hat. Heidi from wardrobe is distraught, and is perhaps dismissed with a meaner spirit than he intends.

If you think about it, no soldier is going to stop while facing almost certain death to take off his hat, or to put it on again. Caroline goes up to the director, who is now taut with tension. A quiet word which she makes sure no one else can hear, but her body language spells calm, no-nonsense reason. Nothing's said. Tom shoots the scene both ways – hat on, hat off. Let the editor sort it. Caroline, once again, has sorted Tom.

On this, the official day off, she's up in her room, writing up notes, intricately marking up the script line by line for the editor. She must save hours of post-production costs which, budgeted at £138,000 excluding music, is no small gift. It isn't as if she doesn't have an enormous sense of fun. Dinner with Caroline telling tales of her thieving childhood on a council estate to the despair of her over-worked Irish mum is to revisit Dave Allen. She has the same mix of deadpan charm and wicked sparkle.

Because of the paperwork, there's no Caroline in the posse which gathers early on the day off for the adventure by train to Agra to see the Taj Mahal. At Diggi Palace Hotel, the Russians plan to pass their rest day without moving from a table on the lawn after a night which involves at least a bottle each of whisky and rum. A friendly football match is on the schedule in the Trident-Hilton gardens. Halfway through the shoot is a low point and there's a palpable irascibility, much of which is anticlimax. What could have been a mess, or at least limp, was pulled off in triumph against the odds and the report from London is that the rushes are thrilling. No one sets out to make a terrible film, but this see-saw uncertainty explains why they so often do. Until it's up there on the screen, it could as easily have failed as worked.

The irritability is also the inevitable effect of the intensity in which it was accomplished. For weeks everyone has been living at their emotional nerve-endings. Where the rubbing up goes the wrong way, people now get seriously pissed off. Also, this halfway mark sees the arrival of a pride of wives, husbands and partners. Perversely, the interruption is both welcome as an idea and resented in reality. The unit's closeness is diluted as all manner of unknowns mill around at loose ends. Going home again, although a month away, is becoming real and certain attachments are clearly being re-assessed. 'On location doesn't count', the industry slogan, works about as well as 'one size fits all'.

For me, it's a chance to look back and try to make sense of the past weeks. Some lessons are self-evident: that budget constraints and the bottom line have fudged the fine line of authority between production and the creative crew. Many decisions that might once have been the responsibility of individual heads of department are now made by the production department. If feature films are still (mostly? occasionally?) a director's medium, in television it is the producers who have raised the money and hold the ultimate power. Appointments and choices that might have been made once by the director or production designer have been purloined by the co-producer, the slender and piercingly tough Julia Stannard. Claire the costume designer, for example, was Julia's recommendation to Malcolm Craddock, not Tom Clegg's.

If Malcolm as the creative producer has the muscle, it is Julia who holds his purse strings. Fair enough, perhaps, considering that her personal success or failure will depend largely on her ability to pull this production through on budget. Lucky Malcolm who, as scapegoat on the old *Sharpe* films, had to bear the brunt of crew resentment. Julia takes the flak now for the penny-pinching, and he's free to limp around tortured by bouts of sciatica, and the hollowed look of the sacrificial leader on his face. 'This hurts me more than it hurts you' is the message. He is clearly a man who looks back on years of being a ruthless son-of-a-bitch in a ruthlessly competitive industry, and reaches inside himself for redemption.

As always, resentment isn't entirely about money. It's about a perception common to all creative institutions that production people are 'the suits', 'the grown-ups'. Those who make it happen are supersensitive to any suspicion of being pushed around as grunts. Some of it isn't anyone's fault. There's resentment about the constant nagging from on high for written 'Assessment of Risk' sheets which have to be completed for each scene. Many veterans still regard them, 10 years after their introduction, as buck-passing and box-ticking. To the creative types, it's a symptom of a suffocating and increasing bureaucracy pinning them down: 'the business' is now 'business'.

But there's also a feeling that decisions are made increasingly by those who don't have to (never have nor even know how to) carry them out. To some extent, it's a valid criticism. The production staff on *Sharpe's Challenge* do have a tendency to bustle around like White Rabbits laden with folders invisibly marked 'Important'. The paradox is that ultimately *Sharpe's Challenge* doesn't depends on budget print-outs but on what appears on the screen.

Nevertheless, although Tom Clegg is the centre of authority during shooting, overall, it's equally invested in the private weekly meeting between co-producer Julia, her close friend and production manager, Emma Pike, the production supervisor, Alex Sutherland and the gentle, green-eyed production accountant, Maxine Davis. It is to Maxine that crew hand the thick bundles of receipts in Hindi to reconcile with each department's allocated budget. Hundreds of transactions each day to be pulled together into detailed weekly cost reports against a budget locked firmly tight. She's the one with 25 files on the go and money coming in and going out in about six different exchange rates. (Relief all round when the rupee drops a bit against the pound.) Even when it's about bookkeeping, it's about relationships. 'I like to go out on set and I like people to know who I am – I think I need to be accessible for this to work.'

Once Maxine has projected forward and flagged possible areas of concern, it's up to Julia to decide if and where cuts will have to be made. Thus at one point Garth Inns of SFX was going to be sent home to England, leaving Tony to cope with burning villages and massacres in Samode, while at the same time getting ready to blow the wall again at Jaigarh Fort an hour and a half away. Garth's reprieve came one day before he was due to board the plane home and, in some complicated manoeuvre, it involved his volunteering to go off salary for five days.

His banishment might have had something to do with the £18,000 Tom the designer is going to have to spend to build Wellington's library from scratch in a deserted palace building at nearby Chomu, after the prince finally reneged on Jaipur's City Palace as a location. Well, £18,000 cut to £15,000 by Julia. The tussle between management and workers is no different here than in any beleaguered industry. While Malcolm might care to say that people have cut their usual fee or salary because they want to work on such an exciting project, those who admit to having done so say it's because there is so little work around in this last year of the tax breaks which have coddled the British film industry.

What has emerged above all from the first month is how the sheer endurance and inventiveness of the crew depends, in the end, on the interweaving of personalities. Any film school graduate might be able to master the techniques and skills but these are taken for granted. Interestingly, they aren't what Malcolm Craddock even bothers to mention when discussing the team hired. 'I've chosen people very carefully who won't crack under the strain,' he says. What film school doesn't teach, and perhaps can't, is that, where it counts, filming is about character. Where relationships work, the sum is greater than the parts. When they break down, something always goes wrong and talent alone can't save the situation – everyone has to pitch in and it usually means throwing money at it, clawing it back elsewhere. I am often reminded of DOP Nigel's words: 'I hope I am hired as much for who I am as what I can do.'

So to offset creeping mid-stage jaundice, I spend the last night shoot, the last we spend at Jaigarh Fort before the move to the desert at Samode, sprawled in an extravagant tent, rocking away to make-up's eclectic collection of CDs. I loll about watching Marella, Marc and Tori pack up £30,000 worth of wigs, £8,000 worth of facial hair and £20,000 worth of assorted other kit including printer, digital camera, laptop, rollers, hairdryers, tongs, stereo, £500 brush sets, eyebags, teeth, assorted severed heads and limbs, silicone tie-on wounds of a ghastly nature and about 400 assorted jars and bottles.

It's flattering to be asked to pin bits of hairy stuff onto a travelling board. A small sign, perhaps, of acceptance. In her domain, Marella is the head girl you long to please (as indeed, she was at school). Almost all of the kit belongs to her personally and is kept in her London basement. Because she's scared of spiders, Marc's role is to go down and bring it up each time they set off to work. It's always assumed that make-up owns its own tools and brings them to work. Historians call it 'labour aristocracy', which explains why the costume department, which would seem to deserve more respect, is the lumpen proletariat by comparison.

Marella is paid £50 a week 'box money' to use her own stuff on top of her £12,000 allocated budget, some of which went to streaking Sean's ragged hair at Daniel Garvin and blonding Lucy's at John Frieda's. ('We don't ever colour artists' hair because of insurance complications. What if it goes green?'). As a result, Princess Lalima is wearing Martine McCutcheon's old wig and one of the Russian stuntmen is wearing

Amanda Burton's, thereby saving *Sharpe* about £4,000 in wig-making fees.

Right now, Tori is despatched to take charge of spraying blood and creating wounds on the many dead and dying of the Forlorn Hope, while toting her heavy make-up bag around a hill which hardly has a foothold left in the crumbling soil. This is not an easy, flighty ride, Marella points out tartly, 'We literally climb the hill and eat the dust and the cow-dung smoke.' Tori Robinson, who looks like a young Susannah York, is officially a trainee but has taken over the organization of make-up for the hundreds of extras. It's the natural authority gene again. Marella zeroed straight in on her two years ago in her class for Brush Strokes, the £6,500 four-month make-up course run at Shepperton. After years as lead singer in a rock band ('We did the Dorchester, the Grosvenor House, we went to Milan and Paris …'), make-up was Tori's mid-life crisis. She was 24.

Former lives are an eye-opener: it's as if rebellion and experience for its own sake is the best qualification for film work. Tony of Special Effects is the son of an engineer. His rebellion took the form of leaving home at 16 to become a hairdresser in Eastbourne, before going on to work as a music freak in a record shop. This was followed by stints in the perfumed costume departments of the National Theatre and the BBC before someone noticed that he was handier fixing electricals than ironing shirts, thereby launching him on his path of SFX destruction.

Marc drifted through two years of wigs on the national tour of *Phantom of the Opera* before running into Marella at a drunken wedding reception. She called him in desperation for the last three weeks of *Boadicea* in Romania. 'We got on like a house on fire. At the end of day 1, she said "OK, you're working for me now."' What she needed was speed and teamwork and Marc delivered both. On set, they stand by for the last-minute call: 'Checks, please'. 'You should anticipate checks,' says Marc, and then disapprovingly, 'Make-up artists who are too busy chatting and flirting on set keep the cameras waiting.' So Marella and Marc finish one another's sentences, gossip together endlessly in the catering tent, shop and hang out together in their time off. Both single, they're not instead of family. They *are* family in a scattered, interrupted life. Such solidarity explains why they're by far the cheeriest team on set, and why they're such favourites with Graham Norton back home between films.

The key is to make sure a unit isn't standing around waiting for an actor to emerge from make-up while keeping the atmosphere relaxed. Fancy hairdressers from salons in Jaipur get hired and dismissed after a day. They can't take the pace. And besides, most of them have no idea how to 'dress' hair for period work. 'It's about letting the hair fall into your fingers, letting it curl where it wants and pinning it there. All most of them are taught is cut, cut, cut,' says Marc with exasperation. Neither can the local Indian hairdressers take the discipline of reproducing the look Marella has designed and captured in her meticulous set of continuity books. Filming these days is as much about systems organization, paper work and wall charts as doing the job itself. Given the jumpy way shots are scheduled across time, it would be all too easy for an actor to enter a room looking one way, and exit weeks later looking confusingly different.

So tonight Marella and Marc tackle the debris in the tent in between making up the lead actors and turning Russians into Indians. The look is rugged: this is India, dusty and dirty. The soldiers have marched hundreds of miles, hair is slightly awry, faces smudged. Sean is never clean shaven, always stubbled with a day's old beard. Where years ago, Lucy would have had the classic look of the 30s or 40s Hollywood, everything immaculate, realism (or some approximation to it) is today's fix. Think a cross between Kate Moss pre-rehabilitation and Esther Rantzen in *Celebrity Come Dancing*. In theory, on screen, it should look as if women aren't wearing make-up at all. It's an intricate mix: historical authenticity matched with an awareness of contemporary, product-led styling. Lucy's Celia is still too 'girlie' for my taste but everything's a compromise.

Where make-up stands in the unit firmament is clear from any comparison of Marella's gorgeous, air-conditioned tent with co-producer Julia's overcrowded box-like room and Tom the production designer's windowless, airless office, or the way the sound and camera departments have to make do with lock-up buses, let alone Tony and Garth's special effects' studio – the tented hole in the wall with its one naked light bulb. Interestingly, facilities are one area no one complains about. That's because everyone understands the emotional charge of Marella's fiefdom.

It's about touching the flesh and soothing the psyche. 'To change some-one's image is a painful process, so they're afraid until they trust me,' says Marella. 'Sean, for instance, didn't know me from Adam when he arrived but he has to get on with me because, in the end, I am going to look after him.' Marella is as much confessor, nanny and mother as illusionist. Make-up is the last place actors will be before walking on set. A cold, business-like room and there will be unhappy actors. 'If actors aren't at peace in here, they won't be comfortable on set.' It's all in the laying on of hands: some need fussing, some don't. Some need an emotional 'cuddle', others bracing.

Watch Sean being 'checked' on set by Marella. He stands still looking somewhere in the middle distance, rather like a child distastefully allow-ing his snotty nose to be wiped – which often he is thanks to the burning cow dung and dust. 'Actors? Your best friend until the film's over and then you never hear from them again,' says Marella. Perhaps that isn't always true, but almost. Once again, it's as much about relationships as skills, about being able to judge people at a glance. 'You have a great time doing this,' says Marella, 'until you see it on screen six months later and wish the fuck you'd done something different.'

Early in the morning on the second day off, I ride out of Jaipur into the desert at Samode with Rajput Ram Pratap Singh, who wants to see where his polo ponies will be stabled and working. We slog through deep sand, which was once a river bed during the years long ago when there were proper monsoons. Trees and bushes cling to life in the splintered cliffs around us. No sound but for wind and birdsong as the sun creeps into the valley over the velvety Rajasthan hills. A band of black-faced monkeys has been tracking us. The world is utterly still. This land, says the Rajput, makes you one with it and with the God who gave it.

This is why filming seizes the spirit and captures all those talents: there's no real money in it for the most part, almost no one has a pension put by. It's a hard grind, long hours and often months of unemployment. But it transports those who work in it to places, both outside and within themselves, that most would otherwise only dream about. If only for a brief while, it makes everyone more than they are. Next week, this empty valley will be destroyed for a short while: even now catering tents are going up, tractors gouge out the hillside. And when we've flown away home – a thought I can hardly bear – next year's monsoon ('God willing,' the Rajput reminds me) will wipe out all traces, as if we were never here. The first act is over.

Bottled water only for the Brits and Indian chiefs

Caroline O'Reilly: 'the knowledge'

The Author Pays a Visit

On 29 November, with only three weeks to go until the end of the shoot, the whole unit moves to Samode. The base with tents, trailers and Dr Panya's ambulance is at the top of the valley. It's half a mile walk through deep sand to reach Chasalgaon Fort in which Toby Stephens' ruthless Captain Dodd massacres every man, woman and child, with the young Sharpe the only survivor. Be sure there has been, shall I say, a lively interest among the blokes in how Sean is to be passed off as a 25-year old.

Beyond the fort is an Indian village, site of another ghastly massacre, and to one side a camp of white tents, the British army's lines. The valley is surrounded by crags over which there are sublime sunrises and sunsets, and, far off, the whine of a furniture factory. Alistair shudders at the sound, but he'll know far worse once the Jaipur drivers hit the Jeeps, and regularly get stuck in the sand for which their recourse is to rev the engine as fiercely as possible. Luckily for him, the crew give up on Jeeps and use camel carts to haul the heavy equipment in from base.

The fort could have been here for hundreds of years: Henry Harris and the stick-thin labourers from Mumbai finished it yesterday, complete with scuffed-up parade ground, a mighty flagpole and a cookhouse stained by years of careless use. Is it 'real'? Does it matter? Had it existed, this pitiful outpost would have long ago crumbled. That's the brilliance of Tom McCullagh's design. He stood in the shoes of the British officer unlucky enough to have been posted here, and reckoned that he would have had to build the fort with whatever was to hand. As a result its clay-moulded mud walls blend into the valley, an illusion of power, and a reminder of how feeble such power can be. 'I had the image of that hot track across the desert and I just sketched it the way I thought it should be,' says Tom. He then, of course, puts the credit on Henry. 'I sketch ideas and he makes them real. He's a lovely man who doesn't get excited – he's my kind of personality.'

The valley affects everyone differently. The Great Bagh Hotel crisis distracts most people. We are in the middle of nowhere. The nearest hotel is the Samode Palace Bagh, a tented summer retreat attached to the rich hotel at the top of a nearby hill. The Bagh is hardly camping at Bognor – this is luxurious roughing-it. There are walled cottages – only the roofs are tented. There's a sunken swimming pool under cover and elegant terraced dining. But not only has the winter cold bitten deep but a shortage of rooms means that people will have to share: another of those delicious

Bernard (left), Gareth and Alistair at Samode

tests of hierarchy as it leaks out that one or two, maybe more, have wangled rooms by themselves. Feathers ruffle, voices squeak, outrage fires across the production office set up in a dump down the road. There is a choice, though: stay at the Trident-Hilton and make the hour and a half journey each way. Trust Tom McCullagh to take it without a fuss. 'I just thought I can't be bothered to get into that. It was easier to stay at the Hilton.' Nevertheless, in a unit given to such palavers in direct relation to their toughness at work, this becomes one to end all such palavers.

This is tricky. I'm paying, so could take my own room. But then I would be one of 'them'. In the end, I book into the lavish Samode Palace Hotel, and slip in and out of the Bagh, grateful to have a bolt-hole from the evenings around the campfire. It's certainly a relief to escape the exuberance of one of the crew's favourites so drunk that he almost topples into the burning logs while roaming the circle calling for a blow-job. No-one shuts him up; he's an actor.

Not everyone gets caught up in the Great Bagh Crisis. Alistair and James continue life at the Trident-Hilton and on their own island, savouring the valley's peace. Tom McCullagh is often to be found standing outside the fort, marvelling at the solitude and beauty. Malcolm Craddock, who has doubts enough about 'what we're doing to the world' and the uncertain existence of an afterlife, confronts the contradiction set up by the violence and death his film is glorifying. Fortunately for his already troubled soul, he doesn't see the herd of polystyrene tea and coffee cups blowing for eternity across the desert at the back of the fort.

Tom Clegg, driven by the realization that he's now over the halfway mark, is becoming even less of an elf and more of the class bully. He'll reshoot a sequence because an extra doesn't drop to the ground exactly as commanded, or guns aren't raised to the same inch. He lams into Gareth the stunt co-ordinator because the Indian 'soldiers' don't die with sufficient drama. 'It's going to be all right,' says Gareth in deep Welsh gloom, 'but I'm casting myself on the rocks of destruction.' Tom turns a small inner corner, though, and apologizes to some of those he's torn apart, trying to win them back with charm.

To one side of the fort, a small Indian village of round huts with thatched roofs is set out around an enormous thorn tree. Henry and the carpenters have built these in order for them to be burned down. The wind keeps changing in the valley but Tom Clegg wants the smoke to rise in exactly the direction he dictates. He wants it blacker, he wants it higher, he wants it steadier. As a general rule, it's best to keep out of his way at Samode. On the bright side, even the nay-sayers have to admire the solution for the anti-ageing of Sean. No attempt to pretend he's anything but a worn, abused, weathered British private: the only concession is a mane of long, unkempt hair trailing his collar. A gutter boy such as Sharpe would surely have looked like this after years of army grind. Authentic, for sure.

At least the noise of Jeeps, of tractors grinding through the sand and of Indian crew chattering endlessly in the shade no longer sets nerves on edge. Slowly, the message has got through: no one's going to change India, and some don't even want to. So the commands 'Quiet for a rehearsal' or just 'Quiet for a take' are given more in hope than expectation.

Slowly, despite themselves, the valley heals the spirit of the crew. People are drawn together again as they shiver in the bitter pre-dawn cold of breakfast in the catering tent, breathe freely under the huge noon sky, compare vomiting patterns. 'At this point,' Gareth announces, 'I'm looking forward to going home not for any other reason than it will be nice not to have diarrhoea for a bit.'

A film crew is a like a pack of animals. It has to read intricate body language across distance, keep a wary, panoramic look-out for danger, and it can spot enemy 'suits' at a sniff. If there's one thing that makes it stiffen with tension, it's the presence of the latter. There's a visible resentment of the newest arrivals shepherded in by the jovial and talkative producer Muir Sutherland, newly returned from London. Even the band of stunt goats has been made more welcome. The walls of the fort are as symbolic as functional. They have banded the crew together again, but also shut out those they deem to be 'foreigners'.

The resentment of intrusion shows in the fastidious way that people step round the visitors on the way to equipment and then have to go straight through them to get back. The crew are pretty dreadful about avoiding actors' eye-lines during takes but they manage never to catch the eye of the line of well-dressed civilians clustered around a tall, straight-backed man with cigar, sports clothes and floppy nursery hat. Not a smile in his direction from the workers. It's assumed he's 'money' and therefore unwelcome – ironic enough considering they've been bellyaching about that commodity for weeks. And since a film set doesn't have the least social niceties (heaven forbid that anyone except Sean should be offered a chair) and no one ever introduces anyone, the brief presence of Bernard Cornwell goes un-remarked until it's too late.

The thought occurs later that it might have been nice to stop for a second to introduce the writer of some 40 plus historical thrillers including the 20 *Sharpe* novels, with another, *Sharpe's Fury*, on the way. Without him, no one would be here. A round of applause might have been tasty. As it is, the only such cheer is for one of the more popular supporting actors who is put to death when the pistol finally goes off on the ninth take.

The Rehearsal

Nothing is as cruel as this popularity contest: actor after actor is to die during the next few days without so much as a 'well done', let alone the spontaneous round of applause accorded the rotund Nicholas. As for the annoying Indian child actor with his Mrs Worthington of a stage mother, even the tender boom operator James was heard to wish he would die sooner rather than later. Since no one minds about anything except that the boy should live and perish affectingly, his brattish behaviour has been treated with the patronizing attention one usually lavishes on other people's ghastly pets. The sad fate of most child actors was laid out on his page as clearly as Cornwell has laid out the complicated, villainous and yet honourable character of Richard Sharpe ('He's a villain, but he's on our side', as Bernard puts it).

In a recent *Guardian Books* interview, the journalist asked Cornwell whether or not he harboured 'an ambition to write something weighty and serious', which is a bit like asking Jane Austen whether or not she secretly longed to tackle the Social Problem Novel. He's a storyteller. While it's an achievement to have sold over 20 million books around the world in this day and age – or any age, for that matter – his real satisfaction comes from doing what he always dreamed of as a small, unhappy boy reading CS Forester's 1930s classics about Hornblower, and enthralled by history, especially military history. 'I think nations are defined by their history. I don't know how the French cope with 1815, 1870, 1940. The English have been extremely fortunate, they haven't had that measure of defeat. When Sharpe goes into battle, he doesn't expect to lose.' What goes for nations, goes for men of course.

Cornwell, who had a horrendous childhood with adopted parents, waited until he knew he had nothing to lose and maybe something to win before tracing his biological parents. 'It's not as if there is a yawning hole in your life – and if there is, it's a bloody dangerous thing to do.' He was 57, had a second happy marriage living in a town with 65 miles of coastline, a small fleet of boats to sail along it, and a regular place on bestseller lists. He wanted nothing of the parents who abandoned him as a newborn. 'I grew up at the point I thought: "It's so easy, we can blame Adam and Eve for all the evil in the world". I'm not into blame.'

It's one of those small jokes life plays that he didn't find books in his cultivated, successful upper-middle class Canadian father's house – a father he is 'very, very fond of'. Why would he not be? In meeting his father, he found his own face and mannerisms reflected in a man who had clearly blocked the fact that he abandoned his pregnant girlfriend after 7 months of wartime romance. The irony is that it was his East End mother, a woman with whom he found little else in common, who had packed the shelves with books – historical novels. His father has cancer now, his mother died last month. Time closes in.

He has written movingly of his early experiences after being adopted by members of a sect known as The Peculiar People. They were puritanical, mean and vicious in the correction of 'sin' and Cornwell hated them. His survival and success must have been driven by that hatred as well as his own courage. 'My one slight regret is that I wasted so much time fighting those fucking Fundamental Christians only to find out there is no enemy.'

Already the comparisons are there with Sharpe, his creation, who was warped by his childhood in the workhouse and driven by necessity, hatred of injustice and an idiosyncratic, ambitious intelligence. It is some surprise to Cornwell that his hero ends up with a gentle, loving Frenchwoman – especially given Sharpe's years of fighting with and his innately English hatred of 'fucking Frogs'. But then Cornwell has been married for 25 years to his gentle, loving American and, for her sake, lives on Cape Cod while writing about a Britain and an Englishness few can any longer recognize nor own. 'If you're an exile as I am, I think to an extent you create the England you want because you're not there.' He also lives in a very patriotic society and doesn't quiver before it any more than Sharpe does. 'I think patriotism is an incredibly powerful force.'

He's a shy man who acquired a dangerously thin layer of hearty, self-deprecating humour as a successful BBC producer on the current affairs programme *Nationwide* years ago. In a tight corner, he has the news reporter's stock of ready, well-polished (and well-worn) stories and sound bites, all the better to deflect attention or, worse, praise. As a result, he has the good manners of a man who uses them to keep others at bay.

Lacking any small talk, he has perfected the opaque blank expression of someone who doesn't mean to be rude but might need to be left alone to think about something else. 'I'm fine with my friends and I'm blessed with many of them but if I meet a stranger, I dry up. I'm like Sean in that respect. I'm completely tongue-tied.' But get him going and a real face emerges from the English flatness and his eyes come alive with warmth – a deep and reflective warmth. He listens, he thinks and engages with ideas: no wonder admiring acquaintance-as-mirror doesn't interest him at social events. Again, any more than it does Sharpe or Sean Bean, both, in their own way, up from the ranks, fighting for themselves on talent alone.

At first sight the quotation of his alter ego in the front of *Sharpe's Eagle* doesn't fit. It is Samuel Johnson's: 'Every man thinks meanly of himself for not having been a soldier'. On the other hand, he has fought his own wars: the childhood, of course, Northern Ireland in the 70s ('the greatest story in the world at the time'), but, more recently, with cancer which seems to have tossed aside his sense of identity. And yet if he has come late to a sense of his own mortality, he has long lived with it through *Sharpe*.

It's still more than all that: Bean as an actor draws on a white-hot anger buried somewhere within him from which he doubtless tries to escape. But it's a match for 'the terrific anger' Bernard owns to writing into Richard Sharpe at the beginning. Perhaps it was a safe place to bury it back then, if only in order to let it go. 'Now I have to put that anger back in': the confession of a man who has won his peace. There was a moment in the filming today which, for Bernard, embodied the bitterness of both actor and character. The young Sharpe has been turned away scornfully by Nicholas's pompous Major Crosby; Sean bites into the *sotto voce* line which follows with molten fury. It hasn't escaped Cornwell's notice. 'I know that moment is going to be brilliant. Sean is a complicated man but he's a superstar and I like him. Whenever I write *Sharpe*, I hear Sean's voice in my head. And I think that's an incredible compliment.'

Just like Sharpe, and Bean as an actor, Cornwell is a chancer. He threw over considerable security as Head of News at Thames Television to live in America with Judy who was unable to take her children to London. Apparently most people told him: 'You'll be mad to leave TV. You'll hate it "outside"'. But when he told his news programme anchor that he'd 'got this idea', Andrew Gardner had the guts to say 'for fuck's sake, go and write it'. Before writing a word, ever the conscientious BBC-trained producer, he broke down several *Hornblower*s paragraph by paragraph and made three enormous wall charts showing how Forrester moved action forward, dealt with dialogue, placed explanatory material, anything which helped to tell the tale. 'I wasn't slavishly copying but I needed to disassemble other writers' books to see how they did it.' That sort of homework lasted for three books. For the rest, the huge library he has built satisfies most of his meticulous search for accuracy.

The result of that revolution in his life was *Sharpe's Eagle*, immediately rejected on its first submission on the grounds no one was interested in reading about the British army. He almost took an initial and measly offer for world rights from Heinemann. What followed is one of Bernard's party pieces worth repeating. He was at a Thanksgiving party watching the Macy's Parade going down New York's Central Park West when a haughty English drawl came from behind him: 'They do this kind of thing frightfully well, don't they?'

He turned around and must have said something inane like: 'Oh you're English. What do you do?' A literary agent came the answer. 'I said I've just written a novel and he said: "Oh fuck" and walked away. So I followed him and said I had an offer from a publisher. "How much for?" "Three thousand dollars." He said: "Then it must be a fucking awful book" and walked away again. On the third encounter, 20 seconds later, I said: "*Please* read my novel" and in a lordly tone he said: "Meet me at the Oyster Bar at Grand Central, midday tomorrow." I did, gave him the book and he phoned me at 7 o'clock that evening and said: "How much do you want?" He got me a seven-book contract and it gave me security for three or four years.'

The agent was Toby Eady, like Bernard and Sharpe, loved by his friends but awkward as hell with almost everyone else. 'As soon as I read *Sharpe's Eagle*,' Eady says now, 'I knew it was going to change my life.' That he is still Bernard's agent, that the woman at HarperCollins who took the chance on a first time, military historical tale teller, Susan Watt, is still his editor, is another thread linking writer, character and actor – that of incredible loyalty. *Sharpe's Challenge*, after all, is based on loyalty as Lt Col. Richard

Sharpe (Retd), sails to India to rescue his friend, Patrick Harper.

The *Sharpe* books might be the more famous because of the television series, but Bernard's cycle on Starbucks (hero: Patrick de Lassan – Sharpe's son) and on King Arthur have outsold *Sharpe*, as might his new series on England's first king – Alfred of Wessex. Since they are all rooted in historical accuracy over different time periods, they might seem to be very disparate. What they are all about, of course, is the coming to terms with and teasing the meaning from myth – Arthur's Round Table, the Holy Grail, the creation of England, the production of his own legend by Napoleon. 'Myth,' says Cornwell, 'is the power of history.'

This is why no attention should be paid to his claim that he's merely an entertainer, not interested in the Big Questions. 'I'm not very reflective – that's very English of me, isn't it?' Rubbish. There is not much that is bigger than the driving forces of society over time. He writes about it in a language and form for readers who might not pick up the academic tomes of *Prospect* magazine's top British 'public intellectuals', such as EJ Hobsbawm or Quentin Skinner.

For all that Bernard tries to close the chinks, to divert, to keep conversation on the table, there's one moment which lingers. It's not, surprisingly, when he talked of finding his real parents so much as his passion when naming John Cooper Powys, author of *Wolf Solent*, as his favourite author. 'He has the most exquisite sensibilities of any writer and an immense love of the English landscape.' Powys also wrote his books as an exile in North America but, and here's the rub, he was a man who hated violence, who loved the earth. 'He'd hate my books, hate them. Quite right too.'

What tangled strands compel a talented man such as this to play down his achievements? The clue is in the admiration he clearly has for Powys as a man who followed his own passions. An early ecologist, he was found on his hands and knees during a drought, desperately trying to rescue fish from a dried-up stream. 'He was in agony over this, in agony.' A pause. 'Well, me? I'd think fried whitebait, wouldn't I?' Somewhere, too early, he was taught to pull back into either denial or camouflage – but then that is the supreme attraction of Sharpe, a man of almost no personal intimacy. Life serves art.

However, another paradox, *Sharpe's Challenge*, although based on Bernard's three India books, is not of his writing or doing. Lucille and Richard Sharpe, according to Cornwell's written version, live on into their 80s, and indeed have the son, Patrick. In the film going on in the Samode Valley, the gentle Frenchwoman has been killed off to allow other romantic possibilities. What will he do about this? And, worse, his next *Sharpe* is set in 1811 – at 50-plus, won't Sean look a bit old for the part? Why not move the action forward? It's the first tart moment: 'I don't write for Sean or for *Sharpe* films,' he puts me in my place as he must have done often in his early school-mastering years. 'My business is putting words on shelves, not pictures on screens. And if I did …' A pause. 'I'd be incredibly disappointed.' His eyes soften and twinkle and embarrassment melts. This is a nice man.

The Star Revealed

Bernard Cornwell is loyal to Sean Bean. He makes a point of seeing everything the actor does. He went to Bean's *Macbeth* when it opened in London, despite some patronizing reviews from the flamekeepers of 'art'. Bernard and his friends agreed in advance to leave at the interval. He not only stayed – put more simply, he couldn't pull himself away – but went back twice. 'Every actor playing it is looking over his shoulder at every other actor who's ever played it. Not Sean. I understood for the first time ever what it was to see a Shakespeare play for the very first time. He was utterly fucking electrifying.' This nice man who believes that life is about pursuing happiness, truly likes Sean, who for the first few weeks of the shoot had seemed to exist under his own gruff, crotchety, distant cloud.

Because of the way everyone on the set dances around what they imagine to be Sean's sensibilities, I have fallen into the trap. What I have seen without realizing it is the 'star' as celluloid, one dimensional, always through other people's projection. I have watched his influence on those who laugh more loudly around him, drink more defiantly, play more self-consciously at being one of 'the boys' around him. Bernard is the first but not the last to remind me that this is a man who also commands loyalty. 'I'm not part of Sean's life,' says Cornwell. 'But I *like* him.'

Bernard's championing of the actor makes me think back to last spring, the first time I met Sean. He chose to meet in his pub. That was a surprise.

Most actors these days insist on meeting in specially booked hotel rooms with publicity hawks in tow. In the early evening, the bar was full of working toughs, the smoke from roll-your-own cigarettes hanging over empty chip bags and beer bellies. A roomful of men in dead-end jobs. Sean came in with their same untidy walk: a careless, unfussed walk that marks space as its own and doesn't expect to move aside for women. Of course he was recognized and of course no heads turned. In the world of laddish Brits, real men don't flinch for stars.

I was told I'd be given an hour; we left when they were stacking chairs at nearly midnight. I was taken aback then, but wouldn't be now, when he told me that he'd left school at 16 with a record of truancy and failure. If he didn't learn much else, he learned 'how to take a knock, how to have a laugh, the codes of honour, doing things we shouldn't be doing'. It's the world he goes back into when he goes home: football, beer, the lads, running to Sheffield to see family and old friends. It's as if it's the one true part of his life. 'It's a bit more real, innit? It's your history, it's memories – it's a thickness around you.' Maybe roots are all that ground him.

Three times divorced, an absent father to three children by two wives, at 46 he was dating a woman half his age. By the end of the evening, his six-pint riff on the wilder shores of his imagination had an edge to it – menace perhaps, mockery certainly. I remember thinking that he had the mind of a magpie's nest: inventive and disorderly all at once. 'My imagination when it's unleashed,' he said at one point 'is like a wild animal.'

I'd found his first film, *Winter Flight*, for David Puttnam's Enigma in which he played Hooker, the military bully. Realized in that small but key role was all the visceral class rage of Margaret Thatcher's Britain. Bean's Hooker was pitiless but, as the film's director, Roy Battersby, put it to me, the work of an actor 'with a big hinterland'. His villains, I discovered when I watched his later films, always had something more going on than being merely vicious, just as his Sharpe has more to him than swashbuckling heroism.

The many contradictions to Sean should have been clearer to me. Because he was weaving around the road, I drove him home and persuaded him to let me in to take a look. He must have hated that. His house is his private place. It gave me the chills: the house is beautiful, but decorator-perfect, cold and hard. The quirky, unassuming bloke in the pub, the one who holds fast to friends and roots, was a ghost in it. It was not the house of a man who was easy to like. I remember thinking, outsider once, outsider still.

And I haven't much liked him since he arrived in Jaipur. Slowly, though, in Samode, Sean comes into sharper focus. I notice that he sits on set for hours; the desert sun burns and there's almost no shade. He never pushes anyone away from the little there is. Not once does he go off to skulk in his trailer back at base. The camera never waits for him. Look around and Sean has always been there, cramped in a chair by a hut, glasses perched on the end of his thin nose which, more often than not, is poking through the script. The thought occurs to me that he's nervous. I remember his telling me in London: 'I'm driven when I'm doing something. I'm not a robot. You always think: "Am I going to be able to do that?" The first day you're shitting yourself, it means so much to you.'

Sean, nose in script

He's not an accomplished rider, but the spirited polo pony Rajput Ram Pratap Singh picked out for him is comfortable with him. The Russian stuntmen are down to spurs and tight reins: they're afraid and their horses grow increasingly distressed under their rough handling. The needle-eyed Rajput tells me approvingly that Sean's horse trusts him. Both the stunt double and the stand-in hired for him have had to be moved to other jobs. Sean doesn't coddle himself that way. He throws himself into action and asks for no mercy. In one scene, he skins the knuckles of both hands; they're horribly scabbed and bruised. While everyone rushes at the first medical twitch to the kindly Dr Pandya, Sean doesn't ask for succour, let alone sympathy. 'It's only a scratch. The Russian stunt guys, they get hurt and they just keep it to themselves,' he says later. 'Better to leave it. I had to put these plasters on and they all fell off so I thought "fuck it".'

I ask him whether he sued when his eye was gashed open with a boat hook in *Patriot Games*. He laughs at me. 'What would I sue for? I just think it's part and parcel of the job. It was an accident. People do this all the time. Yeah, well, I might have felt differently if I'd lost my eye.' Meanwhile, he has a long scar below his eyebrow. 'So what? You hear all the time on American television that you can fall down and you can sue someone for money. I'm not that sort of guy. I can't be involved in that shit.'

But it's Naina who brings Sean into proper focus. And it happens in the following way, so forgive the seeming digression. Rural Rajasthan still runs on a feudal order. In this northern state, ancient traditions defy secular, socialist, democratic India. In his own village of Diggi, old men come up to touch the Rajput's feet and bow before him. But Ram Pratap Singh is 46, tragedy has touched his life, compared to which he calls 'unimportant' the two and a half years he spent in a tough Bombay jail on a charge dismissed when the case dragged its way to court.

Rajput Punya Pratap Karan Rathore, on the other hand, is 25, raised as a prince and protected by youth, his Hindu religion and his own innate belief in the power of goodness. There's a touching dignity to his beautiful young face and perfect manners. He plays down the significance of his wealth, ownership of villages on the way to the tiger reserves, and the family fort he's converting to a heritage hotel. Apart from all that, this young man neither drinks nor smokes. 'No, I don't even know the taste of tea and coffee – and the rest is far off. You're seeking satisfaction from external sources. There are certain things you do not have to be curious about.' So it is a matter of amazement to the older royal Rajput that this young paragon is running around the set, fetching and carrying as Sean Bean's lowly personal assistant. 'Why does he do these menial things?' Naina asks in wonder. Punya's curious about people, that's why.

He goes for Sean before dawn and doesn't leave him until he goes to bed at midnight. For weeks, everyone called him by his surname, Karan, because Punya was thought to be too hard to pronounce. It was a careless way of putting him down, depersonalizing him. The young prince shrugs it off. 'They were indifferent to me. I have my own self-worth, it's not important.' Nor, it seems, is the fact that this rich young prince has been put in the most basic hotel down the road with the other Indians, not even with the English crew at the Samode Bagh. The irony is in the awe and subservience with which he's treated by the Indian staff and managers of the Samode Palace, Sean's hotel – the same staff and managers who have no idea why the unknown Englishman has been installed in the Maharajah's suite with its fountain and silver furniture.

Rajput Punya Pratap Karan Rathore, Sean's assistant

The point to all this is that the young Rajput really likes Sean. He doesn't just fetch his Ribena boxes, coffees, teas, nurse his cigarettes and tote his heavy leather bag, he cares for him and about him. There's no question where his devotion lies; there's no wheedling around Punya to get to Sean. Try and he becomes a disapproving prune. Despite appearances, he stands to Sean not as dog to master, but as page to knight. 'It's not hard to work with Sean. He doesn't act like God Almighty and he's not thankless. He expects to be treated like a normal person. I treat it as the first principle of any relationship that you should never judge. One good act doesn't make an angel. One mistake doesn't make a devil. Man is the measure of all things.' So Rajput Rathore, BA (Philosophy), draws on Hindu tenets and Socrates to work with this complicated, many-layered actor nearly as old as his father.

It started badly. During the days Sean didn't show up at Delhi Airport, it was the prince who had to wait around and, as a result, missed the Festival of Lights with his family. To Sean, he was just another assistant. He hadn't interviewed Punya himself. 'I can't do that. It's so embarrassing.' Perhaps the thaw came early once Sean realized the implication of Diwali and started to apologize profusely. Perhaps it came when Sean was ill and Punya stayed in his hotel room, taking him to the bathroom, catching him when he fainted. 'I have done those things for my grandmother when she was sick; when my mother is ill, I massage her head – it's the way we are brought up. But Sean was aware that he was looked after and that's when we understood each other.'

So now, when you see Sean, you see Punya. They hang together; the older man looks terrific, his face has emerged from its shadow. His natural warmth is even poking through. Sean started calling Punya by his correct name as soon as he got better. On the night Sheffield Wednesday play Sean's Sheffield United, they drive together to the internet kiosk in the ramshackle village of Samode to tune in on Daragh's wi-fi gadget to the whole 90-minute game. 'I believe in Sheffield', Sean said in that pub long ago and far away. 'That's where you come from. That's where you can be who you are. And that gives you the ammunition to face the world.' Sheffield as fort, shutting in and shutting out, protecting the outsider at his rawest.

Anyway, Punya didn't start off liking Sean; it has been earned. And it speaks more loudly of the actor than all the coldness, let alone the 'naughty boy Bean' stories floating around the set. It's as if, in producing this larger-than-life, golden calf image of the star, others live in its glittering reflection. What it must produce in Sean is loneliness. Yes, he can seem shy, aloof even to his nightly drinking mates on the crew: 'It's easy to talk, it's harder to listen. I like people who can listen rather than spout off.' Still, it's odd in an actor that he rarely reaches out to others; not even a hand on an arm or shoulder.

In a profession which cherishes its tyrants and flaunts its temperaments, his reluctance to engage works against him. He's never been 'hot', just continually working. The watcher is the lonely one, though, and he's a smart man who lives on his instincts. 'People are sycophantic – I'm aware of that,' he says when we finally sit down together in the Samode Palace courtyard. It's dusk and it was a long day in the desert but he's gentle and quizzical. 'In Western society, people are always manoeuvring, thinking about how they're going to look at the end of the day. People have got hidden agendas, other agendas, it's a puzzle to me. I've got some good friends and they tell me how it is. It's not always nice to hear the truth but they're straight with me. And Punya – well, he's brutally honest.'

As few others are with him, even here. Malcolm Craddock who's 'very, very fond of Sean', and looks on him as his 'gem in the crown', is concerned lest I upset the star. Well, I do. But he doesn't get up and walk away, although tempted to. Instead, he engages, is reflective, even apologetic about some things. He didn't show up on time? 'I was busy. I was doing something. I just felt I'd have enough time to get myself together. Then there was a cock-up with my passport.' The schedule was rearranged around him? No one told him: 'I was totally unaware.' The panic over finding 'Sean's second pillow' for the trailer? He didn't know, he does remember remarking there was only one. 'They sent out for one? No one told me. That's a bit sad.'

The drinking is one thing he doesn't apologize for. Understand that he and supporting actor Peter-Hugo Daley have polished off the hotel's entire month's supply of Guinness. 'It's a day off; people can do what they like on a day off. Why shouldn't I? I am sure there a lot of actors worse than me. That's the way I am. That's the way I've always been. In the scheme of things, it's irrelevant because at the end of the day, we do the business.' I tell him that tourists were photographing him by the Trident-Hilton pool on the day he passed out. Quick as flash, he comes back: 'Not passed out. Sleeping.' And: 'Cheeky bastards.'

But Sean wouldn't still bring the intensity he does to his acting at nearly 50, if he had been embittered by the cheek of others, by slights and disappointments. No actor, however grand, is exempt from rejection. After the *Sharpe* films came to an end in 1997, he was unemployed for nearly a year. 'I couldn't get any work.' When he did, it was the small, low-budget film, *Essex Boys*, a part which he imbued with merciless, unredeemed violence. 'I've felt envy. I've been pissed off that I didn't get a job. It's worse when you get down to the stage there's two of you, and you still don't get it. I'm still competing. A lot of roles came to me only because other people turned them down. I know I can do it – but just give me the chance.' A very Sean Bean smile as he hears himself. 'I know every actor says that.'

It's interesting to see which stories a man tells – with stars, it's almost always flattering. Themselves as friends of the great and good; themselves pulling down gold dust from thunder clouds. The acting and the performance never end. Sean's stories aren't like that. Because he worries about evil and the presence of a benevolent God, he tells me about the time he went into an old church and, sitting there, felt strongly that someone had been there before. 'I like to think there's a force that's preoccupied with this earth.' Not the memory of a 'lad'. What about his acting past? Well, he remembers getting called for *Coriolanus* at the National Theatre and smacking his lips about his part as Aufidius. 'I didn't realize until I got there that I was just the understudy. I thought: "I can't do this for two years, I'll die." I didn't make a fuss but I rang my agent and said, "Get me out of this." That was pretty demoralizing.'

It might seem that *Macbeth* all those years later was his chance to 'show the bastards'. In fact, it was more personal than that. The rupture of a long-time marriage, the crash of another: it sounds easy enough in this industry. This unit is full of fractured families and men who can't imagine staying still. But Sean holds tightly to the past. He doesn't let go easily. Whatever the impetus, it was as if he wanted to go back to the beginning to see what went wrong – or to put it right. 'I wanted to pull back and get back to what it was about as a kid. When I was 16 or 17, I worked every line of *Macbeth*. I found my copy from then and every line has my notes about interpretation and meaning. But I hadn't done any theatre for 13 years and I'd forgotten the rigours of emotion and range. At the beginning, I thought: "Shit, have I done the right thing?" It was hard and it was scary and we were just shitting ourselves. I wasn't confident at first and to tell you the truth, I was pretty crap but once I started relaxing, I could keep the energy going to the end, I was in command and I didn't have to conform.'

Richard Sharpe can't conform either. Indomitable energy and fierce independence: perhaps this is where character and actor unite. Certainly, as older men, both have become more complex, richer in some ways, darker anyway. 'The thing about youth,' Sean says, 'is that it's simplistic.' Some things, I point out, we have yet to see him do on screen: intimacy with a woman, for one. Where there's been such a moment, it's been with men – there's one spell-binding scene in *Sharpe's Rifles* when he picks up old Daniel Hagman from a swamp. 'There is an intimacy between men sometimes that there isn't with women – it's aggression, fight, that's what men have. I just get fed up with this poncing "new man" stuff, servile and sort of fussy. All that farting about is not what women like – not in my experience anyway.'

I ask him whose acting he admires, and I am careful to phrase it that way. He comes back at once – they're all men: 'Pete Postlethwaite, he's so truthful, so honest. I respond to him because I can identify with him. I find him very moving. Tim Roth, Ray Winstone, Gary Oldman – he's almost too good.' Truthful, honest, raw: probably an accomplishment to hold on to these qualities for an actor who works now mostly in big Hollywood productions, but in some way, they're qualities which shut out women.

There's a generic Sean Bean kiss which most fans could do in their sleep (and probably do, there's no questioning the pull of his sexual energy and hunger). He puts his right hand on her neck, left hand just so in her hair etc. And, come to think of it, whenever we see Bean in bed after sex, he's looking away from the woman, never at her. Where's the intimacy in that? And wouldn't it be more natural to kiss women according to the woman? 'Fucking hell,' he says, but he doesn't show how much I must have offended him. He's interested in the idea. 'Yeah, it's like laughter in a way. You think how this character would laugh but I've never thought about snogging that way. I've never thought "how does this character kiss?"' And then the most delicious of smiles. 'I've done a lot of scenes with women and they don't seem too unhappy about it.' For a moment, in the still Samode night where the moon hangs upside down, it's easy to see why.

Once More Unto the Breach

The night Sean and I talk in the Samode Palace Hotel, I decide on the spur of the moment to go back to Jaipur, to Diggi House where I'll feel safe. My equilibrium is rent like an old coat. I can't live at the crew's level of intensity. I remember being asked by countless students how to get into television (nepotism, I answer: it worked for me). Next time, I'll be Mr Punch and say: 'Don't'. It has to be a calling. It messes with life.

In odd moments of being awake and lucid on the drive back, I resolve that I won't throw myself out of the car and that I will remember the driver isn't a fiend. I'm beside myself with tiredness. Perhaps this is why so many of the crew drink themselves into oblivion night after night. Escape at any price. At the sight of the familiar entrance arch to Diggi House, I'm washed with relief and throw my arms around everyone. When I come down in the morning, the Diggi House set say not a word, just the usual glum muttering. I pull my cap low when I next join Alistair Crocker at the sound desk on set. By chance, he'd witnessed my emotional arrival back at Diggi. 'Sorry you weren't feeling well,' he says, poker-faced. 'I've been saving you a bottle of water.'

I travel out to Samode for the last of the fights, and the thrilling sight of the Russians – Pindaris for now – charging full tilt through the burning village on the Rajput's brave polo ponies. Leaving the valley is a wound; when I come back next year and I shall, all of this will have been taken down. Everything will vanish – the fort, the village, the British lines, everything but the polystyrene blowing across the long pampas grass and up into the thorn trees.

After 10 days' filming in Samode, the unit moves back to Jaipur for the weekend. On Monday, we're flying north-west for a week, and most of the crew are packing up the trucks for the drive. Some have already gone ahead to set up the last locations in Mehrangarh Fort at Jodhpur. Only the rump returns to Jaigarh to pick up a few remaining scenes. The last two days of the shoot in Jaigarh Fort throw into the air, yet again, the whole question of authority and co-operation. A crowd is big and noisy, and anarchy runs through it like a flash flood. Hence the weeks' long rupture between production and crew: of order imposed roughly, a bulwark against the ever-present possibility of chaos.

In the chilly winter morning at Jaigarh the unit has shrunk almost to a small knot. With only 10 days to go before filming is over, and the large set-pieces in the camera, many of the crew have been laid off. Who lost whom from their department has, of course, implications about status. Suddenly, Indian assistants who had been ignored for weeks are said to be 'essential'. Naturally, it's more complicated than that. The more open-hearted of the heads of department have, almost against their will, taken their Indian helpers into their family. Tony Augur, kind in spite of himself, has been seen feeding his SFX team 100 rupee bills, as he has the fort gardener's children who live in a dank hole in the wall next to his tent. Thanks to this tough 'death and destruction' obsessive, the tiny boy now proudly rides a plastic bike up and down the dusty pathway and the little girl clasps a garish plastic doll to which she is inordinately attached.

All kinds of manoeuvring have gone on behind the scenes to trim the salary bill. I suspect that the threat to send Garth Inns home early was a tactic to shake loose from Tony's paternal grip some of his Indian special effects boys. In fighting for Garth to stay, Tony had to give up a few pawns. There's grumbling as usual about why money is so tight. The cash flow must be under strain by now, given that most of the money won't be coming in until the film goes out. Wouldn't it be more grown up for the 'grown-ups' to level with everyone? Yes, it would. Doubtless, production think that they have. But everything to do with the budget is still treated as top secret.

Rather like an unreconstructed Dad's wage packet, it's not for the children to know.

As welcome as Maxine's weekly visits are to hand out envelopes with per diems of 5,000 rupees, they do smack of the ritual of pocket money. It's not intentional, perhaps, but it's demeaning. Thus the constant complaints about getting only £75 a week spent by a large section of the crew on vast quantities of drink. As always, money bears the brunt of emotions denied. The steady Indian production team are appalled by the binge drinking (or, another thought, delighted by the sense of superiority it affords them). The English, they say, are the worst of all Western crews in this respect.

The per diem is an easy target for resentment which is all the stronger for its emotional symbolism being unconscious. I'm losing count of the times I hear about the $100 a day per diem on *The Bourne Identity*. Unpopular is the TV veteran who points out that he got only £9 a day when he worked for BBC Wales. Looking on the bright side, at least Maxine remembers who's who. It was interesting at first to see the silent, brutish defiance of crew members whose names couldn't be brought to mind. Heaven forbid, they offer them up lest they sacrifice their dignity – and these are usually the same Brits who can't remember the names of almost any of the Indian crew.

So here we are, a few stalwarts huddling in Catering Tent A at breakfast time. In this still pre-dawn at Jaigarh, there is only a sense of muted companionship, of softness with one another. Director Tom Clegg loses his speed-skating forward motion. Mike Mallinson, the first AD, has a smile in his voice. People say 'hello', instead of hurrying past; information handovers are smoother, more quickly accomplished. Watching the body language as people talk, tension is seeping away. It's as if their bodies know to wind down, to get ready for going home. Intriguingly, seven pages of script will be shot by the end of today, where two, three at most four pages have been the average lately. Not for the first time, I question whether or not there's a critical mass beyond which natural co-operation and democracy inevitably break down – hence the managerial bossiness, the routines, the sense of 'them the grown-ups', them in suits, them with walkie-talkies and us in the dark.

The editing is far enough along in London for the gaps to show, and Tom Clegg's maniacal shooting speed has left time to go back for them. The breach that was stormed at night has been painstakingly reconstructed, in order to be blown to pieces on camera early this morning. Various actors are still to be shot, beaten up and drenched in water. And director Tom is determined to have more spectacular daytime shots of the special effects rockets – the ones based on garden fireworks that have defied most attempts to control their path thus far.

What's left of Team *Sharpe's Challenge* moves over to the steep hill below the newly rebuilt false fort wall. Behind his cool, devil-may-care façade Tony must be a bag of nerves. His 10-year-old daughter, in their new home in southern France, would be appalled by his cigarette consumption. (He swears he will give up on her behalf next week in Jodhpur.) One hand holds his walkie-talkie, the other runs constantly through his long, unsettled hair.

The new gentleness shows in the seeming nonchalance with which the few crew members present meander over to set up the cameras. Tom the director could be an Englishman strolling carelessly along a promenade somewhere. In fact, there is a time pressure on this shot. The sun is stealing up through the mist; its desert blaze will soon flatten the wall and defy the three cameras set up on the hillside.

Behind the scenes, the rigging for the explosion is a triumph of ingenuity and do-it-yourself guile. Three steel mortars, packed with cow-dung patties, bricks and black powder have been sandbagged into the ground. Because the local wiring is so unreliable, the multiple electrically fired charges have been wired individually, lest one doesn't go off. The wires for each charge have been set under the wall which Garth has tied into knots denoting which number it is – a trick from England where there's no point in identifying them with duct tape and marker since it's taken for granted that it will then pour with rain.

Two mighty hinges of second-hand wood and steel have been installed under the wall. Long wires trail from them so that Garth can give a tug when the moment comes. In theory, the charges will set off 'cannon shot' hits and when Garth pulls on the wires, while sheltering under a nearby arch, the wall will obediently tip over one half at a time and tumble dramatically down the hill. Meanwhile, behind Nigel's Camera A set up over on the hill opposite, Tony paces back and forth, the lonely worrier, his normal chattiness silenced.

Well, of course it doesn't happen. After the first explosion, one bit of the wall slips down, and then nothing. 'Bloody wiring', mutters Tony … Long pause. A buzz of communication between Garth and Tony on the walkie-talkies. Silence. Another try. To make matters worse, Rajput Ram Pratap Singh has taken his two sons out of school to witness this historic film moment. The SFX supervisor craves the Jaipur Polo Club fleece which the Rajput still bestows only on the chosen. Tony's now a regular among the Diggi House few who have supper by the braziers set up in the hotel courtyard at a table graced by the woolly-hatted prince with his usual aristocratic command. This is an honour accorded neither to the tourists nor the Russian stuntmen at Diggi. Tony's polo club fleece is another Forlorn Hope, it would seem.

Naina's Indian through and through. His actions are carefully thought through, his reactions are instinctive. In Gareth the stunt co-ordinator, for instance, he recognizes 'my soul brother'. He'd like Gareth to stay on, to make his home at the deserted fort he's bought to convert into a heritage hotel. But Gareth's a circus nomad at heart, albeit a Buddhist one. He fears the temptation, but, like so many of the crew, he fears even more that he'll never stay still, that this life has made him incapable of settling anywhere.

A lot of wire testing, a few more fruitless tries. Batteries changed. Wires re-tested. Problem found. A short in the cable. The hinge had worked beautifully but the pyrotechnics behind the wall didn't go off because of one duff fuse. Bummer. And here is where, at last, the much-vaunted British good manners come into their own – manners revisited so far only in the lingering Rajput's Raj. Ram Pratap Singh clearly expects screaming and shouting. It would be par for the course.

Instead, Tom the director, manning Camera B on another hillside peak, casually sets up a game of 'hit the bottle'. For half an hour, he stands around with the crew, throwing stones at a nearby rock. Burly men fling ever bigger rocks and not one scores a proper hit. Tiny, pretty Menosau

Kevichusa, the Indian clapper loader, who, as feminists would have it, has learned to 'throw like a girl' joins in and is condescendingly tolerated. This isn't a woman's world, let alone a tiny, pretty girl's. A matter of some satisfaction, to me anyway, that when a noisy hit is finally scored, it is Menosau's. Totally in character, the men disallow her hit on the grounds that 'she wasn't aiming'.

Meanwhile, nothing happens on the second, important section of the wall. Garth confers over the walkie-talkie with the calm patience of a man who's spent 30 years in SFX and learned to take death as it comes. Failure isn't in Tony's repertoire. He is clearly gutted and everyone on the hillside knows that. No one even glances in his direction. When he finally gives the nod, Mike Mallinson gives up on his badge of office, the walkie-talkie, and calls the shot as if nothing matters. The remaining half of the wall crumbles magnificently. Eight explosions, rocks flying everywhere. It will look spectacular on film.

Malcolm Craddock, who, for the last hour, has been absorbed in his newspaper, if not actually turning the pages, is thrilled. They've done it. This is what he enjoys; after all the years of working to set up *Sharpe's Challenge*, being here is the fun and excitement for him. So isn't Tony feeling better? 'I'm just thinking about the next job,' he says, all bloke again. An Eeyore pause. 'If there *is* another job, that is.'

Next up, Sean shoots the villain in a hole somewhere which has been turned into a prison cell set by Tom the designer but unfortunately is being used as a through-way by the caterers for the Maharajah's lunch for 500 in the nearby garden. If anyone has reason to play up now, it should be the star. What should be over quickly is drudgery. Sean has to wait in a dusty, concrete alleyway, so narrow that his chair can't be moved out of the sun. The faithful Punya at his side, he sits patiently. His trailer is a short walk away. He doesn't leave the set. His temper never breaks and everyone responds. Not a whinge; the good humour is palpable.

Actor Peter-Hugo Daley is a line-fluffer. His admirers would say that he's under pressure. If anyone is under pressure, it's Sean. He carries this film – or it fails. He's as good as the gold he's rumoured to be getting. Interestingly enough, Sean's salary hasn't been a subject of talk for a long while. He delivers. More than that, he delivers with grace. He delivers here today – line after line, always on target, his focus and concentration never wandering. He might not work out, he might treat his body as if it doesn't matter, but when he works it's with a coiled physical intensity. Yet as he emerges from the set after a take, there's neither twitch nor swagger.

What's more, he stays back and stands next to the camera to feed his lines when it comes to the other person's turn at a single shot. Not many stars do that. More often than not, their time in the limelight over, they disappear and leave the other actor to deliver his big moment in response to the wooden voice of some AD. I realize that I've never seen Sean do that. For every actor, whether the impressive Toby Stephens or the smallest bit-part jobber, he has always stayed to contribute his bits of the dialogue – and, what's more, with exactly the delivery with which he did on camera. As much as he mistrusts journalists and can be cutting to me personally – he does and is – it's hard here not to admire and almost like him. If there are worse behaved actors who are hours late on set or don't show up at all (the Malcolm Craddock Defence), there are surely few more reliable when it counts.

As always, the unit marches on relentlessly. The SFX team is being dispatched back to the scene of the earlier humiliation in the woods to see whether the rockets will fire with enough zing and purpose in daylight. As I walk through the fort, I realize that the false wall has almost disappeared; the mined tunnel has vanished. It's as if they were never there but for a crowd of women patiently taking each nail out of the old wooden planks and putting them into bags. The wood will be sent back to be reused. Nothing will go to waste. In England, it would all have been thrown away or burned. I'm not alone in feeling ashamed to know that.

The British Lines set was down the road cut through the virgin National Forest, now littered with an appalling collection of discarded polystyrene cups and paper plates. With Tony go 36 hand-made rockets, Bharat and Ajay and assorted catering men lumping bottles of water. Ben the second AD is in charge, with Monic Kumar, the Indian Focus Puller as camera operator and in attendance on clapper, Menosau, fresh from her emergence in the hit-the-bottle challenge. As often as she has been overlooked in the past weeks, scampering about hauling heavy equipment without complaint, she is finally being 'seen'. It shows in the flurry of comments about how pretty she is – the only praise the blokes seem to come up with when it comes to a woman.

So, on the now bare patch where once the British Lines set stood, Bharat and Ajay erect the rocket launcher from which someone has stolen the feet. A short pause while Tony hunts around for a few old rocks to stuff under the legs. One of the catering men brings out a kite which he lets fly high above. Ben Burt, in yellow polo shirt and shorts, practises bowling stones downhill. Off-duty football has been vanquished by the Indian passion for cricket, yet another sign that India has seeped through the film unit's hardened, self-absorbed skin.

The walkie-talkies have been long abandoned. A friendly shout is all that's called for. Seven at a time, one after another, Tony, Bharat and Ajay light the rocket fuses. All right, some of the rockets fly sideways into the trees. Others whoosh straight up into the air and down again. But enough swoop across the rocky hillside straight into the camera's path. The early failure happened before the massed crew; victory comes sparsely. But victory it is. And by the time he leaves the next morning for Jodhpur, Rajput Ram Pratap Singh's prize Jaipur Polo Club fleece is in one of Tony's enormous black suitcases.

Padma and the Director of Photography unwind on the last day

TAKE 17

Winding Down

With only five days' filming left to go before everyone flies away for Christmas, the atmosphere changes yet again. At Jaipur Airport waiting for the short flight to the last location in Jodhpur, one crew member is so drunk that he falls over. In order to be allowed on the plane at all, he has to be pushed through security in a wheelchair by Dr Panya, who has criss-crossed his forehead with sticky plasters. When he hears about it, Malcolm Craddock barely contains himself. This is the man who tells me: 'Don't think that I ever had a terrible temper, just a bit territorial and latterly a bit grumpy.' The behaviour of the crew in this kind of public, official forum is very much his territory, and it makes him very grumpy indeed.

No, it's the photographs which signal the difference. Cameras are everywhere, fixing friends for the uncertain future. But the real difference is marked by the other snaps, the ones which suddenly appear from wallets and carry-on bags. Going home is so real, it can almost be tasted. So these snaps are of children who couldn't have understood, when they posed in the last of the long summer days, it would be months before their father would be home again. Tom McCullagh, the designer, shows one of his two sons, the pretty wife who was his childhood sweetheart and the achingly happy freckled face of his young daughter. It's matched by a flurry of such pictures from others.

Young, trusting, smiling faces which in the meantime have gone

OPPOSITE: *Jodhpur below Mehrangargh fort*

through a child's life of mishaps and parties, banged knees and school tests. Christmas trees have gone up, end-of-term reports have come home, presents been wrapped. All of it, missed. Sean Bean tells me that the word he hated in the piece I wrote about him in the *Los Angeles Times* was 'absent', as in 'he's an absent father to three children by two wives'. But isn't he absent? He's here, isn't he? 'It makes it sound as though I don't care, which I do – very much.'

But what can caring mean to a child whose father isn't there for months on end? And, besides, it's hard to imagine how these exhausted, drained men who've been flying for weeks on challenge, excitement and adrenalin will readjust to the small, cosy routines of home, to pushing a trolley round Tesco. All well and good for Blairites to talk of work–life balance but this industry knows no such balance. Would it make more sense to work to pay the bills, by taking a day or two's work at a time? Is it a living, is it challenge enough? The alternative is a high-profile project such as this, with family life experienced down the mobile phone – if it's working. 'When was the last time I got to build a fort?' asks Tom the designer. 'When I was a boy. And I'm a big boy now and I got to build one here. When I go back, if someone asks me to do a contemporary drama with a desk and two filing cabinets, I'll probably burst into tears.' In television, 'the pursuit of excellence' comes with a high price tag, and no amount of Indian pashminas, bed quilts and silver bangles will bring it down.

Nerves are overstretched. The constant drama in the costume department of who's in and who's out – a source of continual entertainment for weeks – is now tiresome. Because next Monday's final shoot doesn't finish until 11.00 at night, there's been talk of holding the traditional end-of-shoot wrap party tonight in Jodhpur. It's Tuesday and tomorrow is the regular day off. Terrible idea, is the general view. The cast party tends to be the time when the verbal Velcro comes off and everyone who has grated unwittingly on someone for weeks tends to find out. There will still be five days' filming to go, and the unit will have to work together … better not. Caroline the script supervisor sums it up best. 'A film unit away is like *Big Brother*', she says, 'Only worse. At least in the Big Brother house, they can get away from each other.'

And it is in this rather treacherous wind-down, that the quiet men come into their own. They're the salve, the glue: soothers and supporters, not inciters. They're like a reliable opera chorus – in the wings or the shadows. There's John Rhymer the Rigger, a sweet-tempered Glaswegian, whose only drawback is a tendency to push Allan Carr's *Stop Smoking*. John has always hung out with Dave Bourke, the 50-year-old Best Boy, but Dave was a casualty of the post-Samode cut-back and has already gone home. Everyone liked Dave, a Brummie with a shy, appealing smile. 'The gaffer's always got his boys with him so I guess his right-hand man is his 'best boy'.' Dave organized the men and equipment for the lighting and has worked with Tom Gates the Gaffer for 15 years. When work's slow, he does electrical rewiring and stuff for 'foreigners' (civilians). But he's unusual among the crew in that film work has been plentiful. 'It's been that long, I can't even remember the name of my boozer,' he told me before leaving. With the artistic lot almost at the edge, the steadying presence is valued

Nigel back to camera; grip Jim Philpott, winner of the Best Butt poll, is in the sleeveless vest

more than ever of the quiet men, direct and uncomplicated.

None more so than the winner of the Best Butt poll, Jim Philpott the grip, whose nut-brown body in his habitual string vest shows the benefits of bench-pressing 80 kgs three times a week. 'Wherever the camera moves, I move it and I don't ever want to be a slow grip.' The grip has one of those invisible jobs which make the flashy ones possible. To watch Jim push the movable camera dolly along a track for Nigel is to watch the most subtle of partnerships. Somehow Jim has to blend his movements to Nigel's immediate, organic and unspoken response to the action or actors. No wonder he loftily ignores all those grip jokes which go something like this:

Question: Why were dollys invented?

Answer: To teach grips to walk on their hind legs.

Jim Philpott knows all the lenses the DOP might choose, the angles a director could consider. 'If the camera's not in the exact position, they won't get what they want.' He doesn't drink when he's filming in case he makes a mistake or can't ease the camera along a track smoothly enough to be sure it won't 'pop'. He has no desire to put in the 8 or 10 years to move up in the camera hierarchy; he earns more than a camera operator already. He owns his equipment – £48,000 worth of it – which is hired out while he's in India, and owns property which is also rented out. He's 25 years-old and he stalks the set, a black cat, lithe, self-possessed, steady and mostly silent. He's an object to be admired, and probably knows it.

And this is when the compliments start to be paid to the one actor who has so far has attracted the least attention because he's given the least trouble. Sean, in spite of himself, is the magnetic centre of the unit: almost no one can resist the force of his presence. But when other actors were reeling around, and almost into, the camp fire at Samode or jousting at hotel bars, Toby Stephens was almost invisible. Friendly to all, polite to crew and actors alike, always there when needed on set, totally prepared, virtually fluff-free – and hardly around the rest of the time. 'When I come into work, I work. You do the job. You get on with it, and when it's over, you get on with your own life. So people don't know much about you if you haven't been in the bar grinding on about your own life.'

Complaining about hotels, for instance, is a given in India: food too slow, service incompetent, rooms too cold or too hot, ambience too noisy or too quiet. It's all about neediness, and its denial: the tougher the bloke, the more constant the grumbling. Not so, Toby. The Ajit Bhawan hotel is noise rampant? Without fuss, he books into the impressive heritage hotel on the hill and offers to pay for it himself. 'He's been a delight to deal with all along,' says Emma Pike, the production manager, who has the unenviable responsibility for hotel arrangements, amid a thousand others. 'He's direct and uncomplicated.' Damning praise in an industry which lavishes its most admiring attention on its imperilled and troubled souls. But then Toby Stephens knows all about those first-hand, and while he may be direct, he isn't for one second uncomplicated. He's masked by public school good manners, self-control and utter professionalism.

At Jodhpur, the high-ups are booked into the Ajit Bhawan, the Maharajah's palace, the rest of the Brits etc into the Ranbanka, supposedly the lesser hotel next door. But the two are connected, we can walk to and fro. I use the fancy gym next door where I find Toby pounding for nearly an hour on the treadmill. The high-ups discover that our hotel is actually nicer, more open to the winter sky; the garden terrace, bar and restaurant have more space to unwind and the staff fuss less. At last, everyone is on a level playing field. It makes this final week even more precious. One afternoon, I finally sit down over a pot of tea with Toby, and bask in his soft-pedalled charm.

His good manners and professionalism are to be expected, perhaps, of the son of Dame Maggie Smith. He doesn't talk about his mother, and I don't ask, but he does tell the story of his time at drama school when it got out that her son was in his year. A fellow student called Matthew Smith started to be accosted by people saying 'I love your mother'. 'Matt was baffled. His mother was a cleaner in Leeds.' It's an elegant way of closing that door, but he also is quick to add. 'I'm not ashamed of it but when people talk about "your breeding" you could end up feeling like a fucking racehorse.'

Fair enough, since he is also the son of that dangerously brilliant actor, Robert Stephens, who died 8 years ago of cirrhosis after a failed liver transplant. The incandescent actor of *The Royal Hunt of the Sun* turned into a troubled, unemployed liability. He walked out of rehearsals, out of productions and couldn't get work for years. A final flowering as Adrian Noble's Falstaff and then as his King Lear, both at the RSC, didn't come until almost the end of his life. So drinking isn't a game to Toby. Acting is work, life is reality and real men don't play at 'boys' stuff' because they get burned.

'I gave up drinking while my father was dying, to try to get him to stop. When he died, I took it up again. I was my father's son in that respect; I could drink and drink and drink and not be sick. My body had no warning signs. But as soon as I turned it off and gave it up, I had a life – the joy of reading a book before going to bed, to make a coherent call without it being bollocks. What a joy.'

It couldn't have been an easy ride on any level. His mother and step-father, scriptwriter Beverly Cross, lived what Toby calls 'a hermetic life in the country'. He was sent to a rough, sporty public school where to be creative was 'poofy'. I can hardly bear that here's yet another of those intelligent dreamers failed by the system. What kind of school was it to have turned out this highly disciplined, clever actor with 2 Cs and a D at 'A' levels? He couldn't have seemed very promising after that: every drama school he applied to turned him down, except for the London Academy of Music and Dramatic Art. 'I was quite on the back foot for a lot of the time.' A slow starter, he emerged as a big enough LAMDA 'star' by his third year to be signed by an agent at ICM and walk straight into a major part in *Camomile Lawn*, the television adaptation of Mary Wesley's bestselling war-time novel. He was chubby, freckled and touchingly young – a long, long way from the taut, lethal Major Dodd of *Sharpe's Challenge*.

In the past, *Sharpe*'s villains have leaned towards the cartoon baddie mould. Even the versatile Mark Strong as perfidious Colonel Brand in *Sharpe's Mission* couldn't get over this one-dimensional, comic cuts aspect. It's a mark of the new *Sharpe* that Dodd is both written as a more complicated character and played by Toby with a venomous, compelling strength, who attracts as well as repels. It's a reminder of Hitchcock's old adage: 'The better the villain, the better the picture.' Toby's Dodd is a formidable British army officer who has known thwarted ambition and been driven by it to treason. The twist comes in the way he identifies with Richard Sharpe, but fails to recognize the possibility of honour in the other man. 'As a villain, you're the reason for the story but a lot of the time they want you to be a proto-Nazi which I can't do. And I don't want to do a whole back-story about "this guy creeps me out, so why is he like this, la la la?" If you can answer that question, he's not a baddie any more. Think of Robert Shaw in *From Russia with Love*. For me he ticked all the boxes. You think: "What the fuck is this guy's problem?" And if you can do that as an actor, you're winning.'

Treason is not an unknown quantity to Toby. Here is yet another actor whose career was 'made' by an agent who found and signed him early, only to be discarded years later when the hard spadework was paying off. 'We had 15 years together but I needed to change the dynamic. We'd got very comfortable with each other and I needed someone pushing me where I wanted to go. It was one of the worst experiences of my life. It was like a divorce.'

It's so ironic: all those successes admired by the chattering classes – anonymous in the wider market place. Being distinguished, admired and an actor's actor counts for little in the part of the business obsessed with image over content. 'One of the humiliations for an actor is people asking "What would I have seen you in?" and you tell them and they still look blank. I thought: "How long do I have to go through this?" I still have to go up for every job and I get turned down 9 times out of 10. I still have periods of not working for 5 or 6 months.' The snake-like traitor, MacLean in *Cambridge Spies*? Who cared? In ratings terms, no one saw it. *Hamlet* at the RSC? 'After doing a year at Stratford, I've spent this year paying for it. I was paid bugger all.'

So, apart from Robert Shaw as the embodiment of the villain, whose acting does *he* admire? Gene Hackman: 'No frills with him, he's just a good actor, a real technician.' Ralph Fiennes: 'He's very, very controlled. He knows exactly what he's doing but he works very, very hard at it.' Penelope Wilton: 'She's like an open wound.' Meryl Streep: 'She's somebody who works hard at it and sometimes you see that. But when she hits, she really hits.' Technicians, actors who act: how different from Sean Bean who looks for a rough, unstudied truth. And women besides. A sweet moment when he actually blushes and gives one of his rare but lovely smiles. 'That's my wife's influence. Most of the time, it's so competitive, you're obsessed and you watch blokes and think "what really works for them".'

And here he is in one of his new, dynamic, high-profile roles, watching Sean Bean, almost an alter ego. I suspect that Sean would give anything to get his teeth, as Toby did, into the searing roles of *Coriolanus* or *Phedre*. And yet Sean garners huge fees as second and third banana in Hollywood productions. It's a strange profession and a mass of contradictions. So what is acting, I ask, apart from a way of paying the bills? He answers: 'It's about an instinctive understanding of human nature.'

It explains nothing about acting talent which is as hard to pull apart as a butterfly. While Toby commands everyone's respect, and has done all through the filming, it is Sean who has got into the guts. On the next-to-last morning, in a painted courtyard of Mehrangarh Fort which rises like a mighty cliff over Jodhpur, there's a crucial confrontation between Sharpe and Dodd. Toby comes onto the set, perfectly dressed and prepared. He grasped early on that Tom Clegg is all action, so there's little time to rehearse. 'After two days, I thought: "Oh, I'd better fucking think about this before I turn up in the morning."' Sean tends to wander up to the set dressed in his crumpled, everyday clothes. He strips off not minding who sees. It's the body of a whippet. No surprise that he didn't pull one vote in the Best Butt poll. But not for the first time, I was touched at the way this star is without vanity. Toby said at one point that he hated actors who are all about 'A Look' rather than content. No one embodies the opposite of that more than Sean.

Dodd has found out that Sharpe is an undercover British spy and had him beaten up. Sean is a mess of blood and bruises, half naked and ugly in his humiliation. But what is clear is how the two actors have hit off each other over the last weeks. Sean is totally prepared, word perfect. And Toby captures some of Sean's visceral intensity. 'I trusted you,' barely whispered and spat at the captive. 'More bloody fool you then,' chokes Sharpe. 'You thought you were better than me,' fury from Dodd, betraying all the back-story Toby won't wear on his sleeve. 'I were born in the gutter, Dodd, and like every other gutter bastard, I know the shit that belongs there.' This is shivers-down-the-back time. It's done in two takes and the first could have served. Cock-fighting, that's what Malcolm called it. It's all about competition, men vying for power in a world of scarce resources.

Early on in the shoot, Eleanor Chaudhuri, the wise, knowing Indian production manager, said of the film business: 'You learn the rules. You play the game. And in the end, you see who has the winning hand.' Toby may have the fuller life; for now, it seems that Sean has the winning hand.

But there's one memory which washes over all the competition and over all the male brutality, which goes under the euphemism of 'boys' stuff', while bringing home the significance of Toby's choice of talking about acting in such human terms. It was a while ago at Jaigarh Fort. Toby had time off and his gossamer-fine actress wife, Anna-Louise Plowman, had flown in with Maggie Smith. The actor was whisking his two women off to see the Taj Mahal at Agra and walked out of the fort, wife on one arm, and on the other his spectral mother with her chillingly familiar face beneath an unlikely baseball cap. 'I thought bringing my mother to India would be a fucking nightmare. It's the most adventurous thing she's ever done. I was so proud of her. And it was wonderful, wonderful.'

Sean as Sharpe: taken prisoner, a scene shot at Jodphur

Check the Gate

In the hotel in Jodphur, the sound team and I are on the same floor and each morning starts with one of Alistair's dry greetings and Jack Dee-like commentary on the shoot's progress. Trains go past my window all night and I delight in their muffled lament. 'Bloody trains, didn't sleep a wink', I hear each morning at breakfast.

In Jaipur, I thought it was madness to move this mini-army across Rajasthan to shoot in another fort. That was before I saw Mehrangargh which rises from the blue, huddled town like an eighteenth-century sky-scraper. Steep, cobbled lanes and long flights of stairs twist mysteriously to the top. In the film, this is the last hold-out of the Maharajah of Ferraghur, where Dodd meets his inevitable end. It's astonishing to think that the film is about to finish on time with only two small, unimportant sequences cut from the schedule.

Naina shows up unexpectedly one afternoon from Jaipur to check on his horses and stays overnight for a Diggi House reunion. On the second day of the shoot, I can't stop shivering (pleurisy as it turns out) and Naina scoops me up and drives me back to the hotel with silvery kindness. My upper lip stiffens: no one with any pride cries in front of a film crew. Wardrobe assistants running in tears from the set in Jaipur taught me that lesson. There's a knock on my hotel door – it's James reminding me that, as an honorary member of the sound department, I must pull myself together. They both turned up when they were far sicker. Really, he wants to know what he and Alistair can do to help. As callous as the crew can be, there is kindness here too. Next morning, I go back to Mehrangargh and ask Dr Panya to keep me on my feet until the end of the film.

So I happen to be around when a storm breaks without warning in a deserted Catering Tent A on the last day of the shoot. There's a small lift which travels up the tall fort, almost to the top. It has broken down, or been switched off. That's not yet clear. The climb seems too hard and long. That the eruption happens in Catering Tent A (Westerners and certain senior Indians) is fitting. For weeks Abhijit the assistant horse-master has denounced the tent hierarchy. There is also Catering Tent B (Indian extras and other crew) and Catering Tent C (any other Indians). Food in Tent A is served on silver tureens. Food in Tent C is served in boxes. Rajput Ram Pratap Singh was concerned enough by the paucity of C to import a cook for the stable boys who sleep at locations with his polo ponies.

Separate tents may be how they do things on Indian films but the Brit/Indian rift here seems to have given it another dimension. Throughout the shoot, hotels have been similarly hierarchical: Sean, favoured actors, senior production in the best hotels; Brits and French in cheaper ones; Indians in cheaper ones still. Abjhijit and Gareth the stunt co-ordinator have grumbled for weeks about the undemocratic way a film unit is run in this, the world's largest democracy.

The first warning of trouble is in the way Eleanor Chaudhuri, the Indian production manager and veteran of Catering Tent A, announces that she has eaten at last in Catering Tent B: 'What a lunch: Marsala fried fish, biryani dry chicken, egg curry and maize. And you had lamb stroganoff – how *English* can you get.' It isn't meant as a compliment. 'In the West, money is faith,' Eleanor once said to me. 'In India, we have a saying: "money is the dirt on your hands."' I remember flinching at the time.

Sharpe's Challenge inevitably raises awkward questions about 'white men as heroes', setting up the British Raj. If this is 'heritage drama', perhaps it's a heritage that sits ill in post-modern, multi-cultural Britain. Is this the Britain we want to export: greedy, exploitative, racist?

Bernard Cornwell's Indian trilogy has a meticulous historical authenticity which, taken on its own terms, rescues the past, fills in the spaces.

Perhaps this hasn't and couldn't survive action-movie storytelling, albeit with beautiful and superior production values? When DOP Nigel Willoughby talks of framing his compositions as carefully as a painter, he's also talking about the British army hacking its way into the Imperial project, as the unit has so often into a landscape which hasn't known a real monsoon for a decade and will have to live with the scars until it does.

Tony Garnett, that extraordinary radical force in British TV drama (*Cathy Come Home, Up the Junction, This Life*), once said: 'The only landscape that really interests me is the human face.' I often wonder whether director Tom Clegg is much interested in the human face. Otherwise, for example, how could he so easily mix 'n' match the Russian stuntmen as Brits or as Indians in brown-face? It's why he's the perfect director for Sean – he doesn't mess with him or over-direct him. As long as Sean hits the mark in the dust and watches out for the camera, Tom leaves him pretty well alone to bring his own stuff to the role which he's made his own. He's fine too for Toby Stephens, professional enough to rehearse inside his own head. Not so good for some others who too easily sway over the top.

It's the ultimate irony: all that military-style organization without which *Sharpe's Challenge* couldn't be made, all that jumping around getting excited about India – elephants, camels, goats, uniforms, forts – and the human face of India sometimes seems to have escaped notice. Is it that the imperial gaze has somehow been directed *into* the text of this film?

For weeks, the Indians have overlooked the way they revolve around the white rings of production power, have ignored the Brits' tactless grumbling about their country. The two Indian production managers, Eleanor Chaudhuri and Rakesh Mehra, veterans of 30 years of feature-film making, have been patronized by young Brits who couldn't have any idea how patronizing they sound. Perhaps power never recognizes resentment biding its time but on this last day of filming, it's as if masks crack in Catering Tent A.

Ramesh Sadrani, the Indian lighting gaffer, is another of those gentle Indians with sad, worried eyes. The firm for which he works supplies the lighting. A key 18 kW lamp has blown out and needs replacing for the final scenes. This lamp, over which a £4 million film might run amok, costs £85.

This morning, Ramesh went to the *Sharpe* production office, sat there for two hours, and left in a huff. The office is frantic at the moment. The entire unit has to be wrapped and shipped off. Ramesh, stalking Catering Tent A, has taken this so personally that he swears he'll turn off the generator.

Eleanor, always so calm, conciliatory, consensual, lets forth on the matter of the 300 rupees. Many of the Indian crew finished yesterday. Eleanor is convinced she is expected to collect from each 300 rupees, representing the extra day's per diem. About £4. Motherly Eleanor couldn't possibly take the rupees from 'her boys'. She insists she will pay it herself. A posse of Indians gather. The atmosphere is electric.

If Ramesh keeps his promise to turn off the generator, there will be no death in the throne room at the top of this oppressive, clammy fort. Why, I ask Tom Clegg, has he left this absolutely crucial scene until the very last moment? 'We're not in the luxury world,' he says. 'On these sorts of things, you're always on a wing and a prayer.' As if all this isn't enough, Tom, as usual, wants more blood: it will be late evening before he finishes. *If* he finishes.

And in the middle of the pretend life, real life has intervened. Two years ago, Malcolm Craddock's daughter died and he was thousands of miles away. He has heard that his father is now dying outside Henley and once again, he's locked out. His passport has been lost and he can't get an exit visa to fly home.

This is a bad moment. For weeks, *Sharpe's Challenge* has lived as a tribe with its own private language; its unity makes of everyone more than they are. Suddenly, everything seems wrong. Familiar faces are perched on the necks of strangers. Everyone is talking of 'elsewhere', of flying away. The ersatz family is being literally torn apart. Outside, trucks are being loaded, tents pulled down, props sold off. Dealers are moving in like so many vultures. This mighty, granite fort rising from the desert floor as a monument to bloodshed and invasion, has its own menace.

The business of film-making as entertainment has never seemed more inappropriate. A film is only the sum of its parts. Those who've been touched by India, question whether there are too many expensive parts here, measured against anything real that the money could be doing. The blow-up in Catering Tent A is a symptom. But of what, exactly? Of the human price of filming anywhere, is the answer.

The Indian crew works as an extended family: when Rakesh Mehra and Eleanor are hired, everyone gets hired – lighting, costumes, designers, sound, cameras, even dear Dr Pankaj Pandya. They're a package. Most of them have been together since *Gandhi* in 1981 and over the years of working together, they have known one another's wives, husbands, mothers, children, all the joys and sorrows of lives shared. When Eleanor's sweet retired husband came to visit, he was welcomed 'home'. When the lawyer husband of Claire, the British costume designer, came, he was another stranger milling around, nicer than most. By comparison with the Indians, a British crew work as so many specks of dust, scattering to the wind after each film, maybe meeting again, often not. It's a dislocated, competitive, casualised working life in which individual bonds dissolve the minute the set is struck.

Even if I come back to Jaipur, to Samode and Jodphur, it will never be the same again. I don't know how to say goodbye. I can't face leaving behind *Sharpe's Challenge*. And right there, of course, is the explanation for the storm in Catering Tent A – nor can anyone else. The private language of the unit is one of jokes and catchphrases; Kingfisher as totem. It has no words, no gestures in which to express this aching sadness – this is about loss, about the fact that this is the end for everyone. The Indians feel it too. They're acting out what the Brits are disguising in dead-pan jokes and the busy work of getting another piccy for the camera. Last day explosions such as this make sense. Anger, resentment or denial: sadness lies beneath them all.

What I have forgotten is that, occasionally, actors and camera rise above everything. And indeed, time and again, the sum of the crew has soared above that of its parts. Today is no different: someone pays Ramesh for the lamp, the generator purrs, the lamps go on. Eleanor isn't allowed to walk up – Ben Burt, second AD, finds a man to turn on the lift. People appear from nowhere to tote heavy equipment up the cobbles to the 'throne room'. And here is yet another of those empty spaces which Tom, Henry,

Barbara, Sunil and Sameer have turned into a bewitching cave. It manages to sum up and explain the enchantment which drew the British to India, and still does: colour, light, harmony, history, brass gleaming in darkness, objects beautifully hand-wrought. As fast as the atmosphere turned sour, so it is healed in the quiet dark evening.

The sadness is here; it's palpable. How can I be so certain? It slides out in small, telling ways. Not once during this evening's shoot does Michael Mallinson, the first AD, have to call for quiet. Voices are so hushed that people have to stand closer to hear one another. This closeness is different. Crew who have hardly exchanged a word except 'cheers' at the bar, are suddenly engrossed in whispered confidences. When they pose for photographs – and cameras are everywhere – they stand with arms around each other, which real men don't do, of course. I'm asked time and again how I am; no one ever asks how anyone is.

The refreshment table has had to be set up a long way from the courtyard outside the throne room. Crew usually wait for trays of coffee and tea to come around – they're not keen on walking, too much of it at the best of times. Tonight they set off together through the arch and come back companionably, cups in hand. There's a nest of a hundred hanging bats in one corner of the courtyard; sooner or later, everyone is taken to marvel at it. Usually, such discoveries are private. When a goat gave birth at Samode, only Marella tried to take people to see the tiny kid in the long grass – and most of the crew resisted her. This sharing and openness makes the bittersweetness of the night almost unbearable. But there is still the crucial scene to shoot. It's difficult to know how the actors can keep up enough intensity for it – it's as if hardness has fallen away from this enchanted place in the fort's crag.

In the very last scene, Sean and Toby fight to the death. Each time Sean emerges between takes, his face is blank, his voice steady – but his whole body trembles. Even now, you have to be really close to see how his hands shake as he reaches for a cup of tea from Punya. He's learned to hide himself almost completely. The received wisdom is that Sean wanders in and 'does his thing', no toll taken. Now I see why he keeps himself away during shooting: he's riven by the effort. Others have drifted away, distracted by the thought of getting to the wrap party, of packing for tomorrow morning's flight, Sean's focus doesn't waver. It's the Law of the Last Inch and I've never respected him more.

And now I understand why Sean Bean is so key. *Sharpe's Challenge* isn't an empty validation of the dead white men from the Raj: Sean's Sharpe is 'other' as, in some strange way, is Sean Bean himself. Richard Sharpe is driven by poverty's hatred of venality, corruption, cruelty and the way men's lives are thrown away for and by money – his is the outsider's view from the gutter, which is the same across time and the world over. It can be read as much as a damnation of globalization as it is of imperialism. Towards the end of the film, Sharpe bitterly says it all, and it will be impossible for some to miss in the words the resonance of Iraq:

'There's me thinking for once all that blood had been about something more than making rich men richer.'

'Heritage drama' it may be and undoubtedly there will be many who watch it for the bangs and whizzes, the reassurance that Albion Triumphs. I shall watch it with an ache, knowing that we constantly live on the shoulders of giants and, very occasionally, television allows us to see from that vantage point.

As Toby's Captain Dodd suffers his last death throes with enough blood running out of his guts to convince Tom Clegg, the call goes out for the last time: 'Check the gate'. Nigel Willoughby pronounces the lens clean. And then magic happens. The Indians, led by the art department's Sunil, step forward with garlands of fresh roses and camellias which they hang around the necks of the actors and British crew. In this still, beautiful, exotic courtyard, anger and misunderstandings, small mean acts and large mistakes are wiped away as Brits and Indians alike, hug and finally look into the faces and eyes of others.

The wrap party is held in an outside 'club' a short walk from the hotel. Where the women have dressed up for the various parties during the shoot, it's the men who have made the effort tonight. Pressed jackets and smart shirts, sprucely laundered, make an unexpected appearance. I assume it'll be a raucous, drunken evening; I cherish its soft and tentative sweetness. The Brits sit at tables lit by glowing candles, and talk more than they drink, glasses held still for once.

On the stage, a traditional Rajasthani 'band' sits cross-legged playing its heart out. Yet another moment of magic as the Indian men get up and dance with breathtaking grace. Invisible men suddenly made powerful and present. One by one, the Indian women join in – and then the female Brits join them, at first with embarrassment and then with careless, generous pleasure. Padma Lakshmi, of course, is a star and no one, for once, resents her beauty. Lucy Brown is captivating and has never looked prettier. I dance and twirl about with Bharat and Ajay of SFX, with Ramesh, now all loose and giving, and, finally, with the wonderful Sunil – it's Cinderella time.

Extraordinary men and women made Rajasthan matter to me. Maybe all these weeks have produced just another few hours of entertainment to fill peak time on two evenings, and evaporate. Maybe, in 20 years, film academics will set *Sharpe*'s heritage among the pulp fiction of the decade – but maybe, just maybe, they will have the wit to discern in it something of the extraordinary spirit that went into its making.

Burning the village in Samode

Cast and crew shot: the last day but one at Jodphur

The Deal

By the time I arrive home in London, everything you've read so far has already been written. Each night, I crept up to my room and relived the day. Even now, India is in my head, more alive to me than the traffic outside my window or the flower stall opposite. Re-reading it, I realize how little notice I took of the actors. Except for Sean and, to a lesser extent, Toby, they came and went on set like so many phantoms.

Filming is an addiction which acquires a momentum of its own. Adrenalin is its own engine. Just getting through the schedule with the budget intact must feel on location as if it overwhelms everything else. What it was so easy to forget out in India is that money serves the film, not vice versa. It's a pity to have lost the old tradition of 'watching dailies' together. In Jaipur, the rushes which arrived every five days were treated as the director's treasury. He alone decided who could see them. As a result, there was a clandestine black market in the DVDs and Tom Clegg would probably burst with fury if he knew how far they'd been circulated.

Perhaps if the producers and Tom had been more open about allowing rushes to be seen by the whole crew, it would have been easier for everyone to remember what they were there for, which, as Malcolm put, was 'trying to do something good, wanting to do a piece of work that people remember'. Out in Jaipur with extras scrambling up hills and the very last night in India ruined by the Great Delhi Hotel Riot (no, don't even ask), all too often the challenge seemed to have become buried in resentment

OPPOSITE: *Major Dodd (Toby) and Padma Lakshmi as Madhunvanthi: the moment of truth*

and Kingfishers. Malcolm Craddock never understood why his best efforts couldn't still the ill-will that rumbled like a storm in the distance.

It wasn't until he was back in London, taking his young son Archie to school, limping up the narrow stairs of his Primrose Hill house to Picture Palace's quiet, homely office on the top floor, that he was hit by the enormity of the last few months. 'Having got back, I thought we must have been mad to do *Sharpe's Challenge*. I was more anxious and scared when I got home than any time before. I thought: "Why do you do these things, Malcolm, why not settle for a quiet sitcom in Primrose Hill?" But the truth is that if I couldn't do this again, I'd be sad.'

Once commitments were made, contracts were signed and financing was in place, there was no backing down in any case. Except that, at any time, almost up to the moment pre-production began in late August, the complicated financing deal could have fallen apart. At least the two partners were experienced and solid enough not to sign Sean's pay-or-play deal until funding was iron-clad. Worse things have happened to the young who still believe the fatal words: 'trust me'.

Muir is frightfully cavalier about all this now the film seems to be home and dry. Either he isn't a worrier, or all those years at the top taught him never to appear so. Perhaps it was easier for him, given his periodic escapes to London, and the protective presence of his Cheshire Cat of a younger son Stuart as executive producer and his institutional memory.

Even now, the financing is bewildering. There were no less than eight contracting partners as sources of financing for *Sharpe's Challenge*: ITV1, BBC America, BBC Worldwide, 2Entertain, Azure Film Equity Fund, HarperCollins, the Royal Bank of Scotland and Sharpe Challenge Ltd. Once Muir and Malcolm put them together (and, for sanity's sake, let's not tally the false starts that didn't come through), it was Stuart Sutherland's responsibility to make sure that all these deals stuck. To put it mildly, it's far from easy to get agreement between such diverse financiers. If at any point any of them had dropped out, the film would have fallen down. When Malcolm was away in India, serving as the unit's avuncular Supreme Court in a Panama hat and Muir was shuttling between Jaipur, London and Madrid, it must have been hair-raising.

In return for two showings in five years on certain platforms, ITV1 came up with a contract worth about £2.5m on delivery of two finished 90-minute films. Only they're not 90-minute films, of course, since 21 minutes of that hour and a half is taken up with four breaks for ads, which is nearly 10 minutes less storytelling time than there was when Russell Lewis was a young scriptwriter. That's either a huge amount to invest or, as Stuart Sutherland prefers to present it: 'When its audience share percentage is spiralling down, ITV is getting a show for £2m which cost £4m to make. What's ITV plc capitalized at? £4.8 billion. What do you think is going to happen to advertising rates if its share percentage continues to fall?' It makes market sense to stake big money on a publicized event such as *Sharpe's Challenge*. Can't stand the ads? How would you feel about drama being funded entirely through product placement, with marketing bosses in the control box or editing suites, censoring scripts in case the wrong piece of dialogue puts off consumers? And yes, it's happened: talk to anyone who has worked in live American television drama.

Hopefully, you didn't miss the reference to 'platforms', which for *Sharpe's Challenge* means one showing on ITV1, and a second on either ITV1, ITV2, ITV3 or ITV4. In the near future this might seem like simplicity itself since deals could end up including pay-to-view, downloading from the internet, to mobile phones, TIVOS, or any other innovation engineers are about to break. Even more to the point, forget artistry for a moment and look at television drama as any other commercial, manufacturing business having to compete in a global market against hungry newcomers – probably best not to think about all those abandoned shoe and textile factories in Britain, refurbished as buy-to-let flats.

'Toiling away in a basement somewhere', says Sky's Dawn Airey, 'is a young engineer whose life's work will make the television we know and love look as antiquated as the electric telegraph does to us today.' Is it encouraging that the legendary Tony Garnett is still toiling away at 70, slender, black-clad, trying to 'love' good programmes out of his young acolytes at World Productions? He calls drama today 'a loaves and fishes operation'. I'll hold on to that thought and try to have faith, remembering what happened to the originals.

It's encouraging for sure that the BBC America channel based in New York came in as a co-producer on *Sharpe's Challenge* with a handsome investment – again in return for two transmissions. The unexpected bonus here was that BBC America not only agreed to pay in advance, or rather on cash flow, but has also bought for transmission the first 14 *Sharpe* films from Granada International. Bernard Cornwell's publisher – and mine – invested to support their author. BBC Worldwide, yet another commercial arm of the public broadcasting system for which taxpayers' fork out their licence fee (yes, another of Mrs Thatcher's can of worms best not to open), paid an advance on distribution rights to international sales for showings outside the USA and the UK, as well as UK non-terrestrial, while 2Entertain, a company 60% owned by BBC Worldwide, bought distribution rights to UK and world DVD sales.

Both BBC Worldwide and 2Entertain sell on behalf of Sharpe Challenge Ltd, and receive a commission. Once their advances are recovered, net profits will go to Sharpe Challenge Ltd and the other investors. The detail is mystifying. If I ran a television network, I daresay I'd also run X hours of soaps and Y hours of regular drama series. Formulaic is predictable and its ratings reliable. All that effort and money invested in a one-off such as *Sharpe's Challenge* and you don't know what you're getting until it's up on the screen.

Only when, but not before, all the contracts were signed, and when it had been agreed which of the investors were entitled to be paid off first since no entity comes at the same rate, did the Royal Bank of Scotland agree to loan Sharpe's Challenge Ltd the money against the contracts to start filming. It's lucky that Malcolm Craddock has what he calls 'a good relationship' – that word again – with the man from the RBS. Nor is this the end of the tale. This already begins to feel like one of those late-night American television ads: 'But wait, there's more ...'

I was standing in the Samode desert, what seems like an age ago now, when I noticed Stuart Sutherland, perfect teeth flashing in the sunlight, with strangers everyone on the unit recognized immediately as 'the money'. Steve Wilkinson, scion of Whitefriars Glass, is 35, has a bouncy set of long curls, the energetic delivery of Donald Trump, and owns Azure, the film equity fund which Malcolm managed to bring in with the last £350,000 needed to get *Sharpe's Challenge* up and running.

Normally Steve's film equity fund has about 20 investors, from whom he raises about £5 million a year. Interestingly, in this the last year of Section 48, the relevant legislation granting tax relief to investors in British films, he has no less than 40 investors in the fund. Gordon Brown hadn't yet promised new legislation at the time but anyway, Steve calls tax dependency 'a dinosaur, a crutch'. He prefers to talk of investing in film in commercial terms as 'risk reward', Azure as a fund with a secure wrap-around tax structure which plays 'hardball with producers' and won't bankroll projects unless his investors gets 'a fast-track recoupment position' – ie, being in on the mezzanine level when it comes to getting repaid and without any messing around with 'creative accounting'. Not that it would happen here. As Stuart bluntly puts it: 'If I fuck Steve over for a couple of thousand pounds on distribution costs, he wouldn't give me £200,000 on the next project, would he?' Or, in Steve's parlance: 'That's a no-brainer.'

There's a catch, of course. If it were that easy to see a drama project as a commercial cert, every film would succeed. Take *Keeping Mum*, for instance, a £10m theatrical film starring Rowan Atkinson, Kristin Scott-Thomas and Maggie Smith in which Azure invested £2.5 million. Steve was particularly anxious to chat to Toby Stephens on set since he'd worked with the actor's mum, Dame Maggie. Trust the ever-reliable and patient Toby to have been charm itself; lucky it wasn't Sean's mum Steve wanted to chat about.

The point is that he's a bit of a dazzler, Steve, and something of a name dropper and, according to him, Azure's investors in *Keeping Mum* had already got their money back. According to the UK Film Council, by the end of January, the film had taken only £1.7 million and still had no American distributor. I'm reminded of something Malcolm Craddock said when explaining why *Sharpe's Tiger* didn't work as a theatrical film: 'There was no interest in it in North America, and the US domestic market is the engine which powers all cinema distribution deals and governs all the rest of the world'. It's that 'mezzanine level' which gives the game away. *Keeping*

Mum might not go in America but it has been sold in enough major territories of the rest of the world for Azure to have recouped.

Steve gets an 'executive producer' credit on *Keeping Mum*, as he will on *Sharpe's Challenge*. So apart from Azure's getting back its £350,000 plus an equity position from future income, Steve himself is entitled to a producer's fee, which he has certainly taken on *Sharpe*, even though Muir and Malcolm deferred part of their production fees as a contingency fund. For all that she was hated for it by the crew (and hate is not too strong a word), it was Julia's relentless housekeeping in India which brought the film in on budget and safeguarded the production company's missing fees.

It took Muir and Malcolm a year after ITV's commitment to put the *Sharpe's Challenge* financing together, and relentless effort on Stuart's part to keep all eight partners 'in bed'. For the sake of clarity (a joke), I haven't even mentioned Julius Pursaill who was introduced to Stuart by his accountant and was persuaded to finance 40 per cent of Russell Lewis's considerable script fee, which is probably at least £20,000 per hour of film. You do the maths. What really strikes a chord is this: Stuart Sutherland is a smart wheeler-dealer, no one's fool and no slouch: at 19-years old he spent a gruelling two years on Phil Collins' 152-concert world tour through 49 countries. In 2000, aged 26, two years after graduating from business school, he co-produced his first film, *The Girl from Rio*, with his father. And, until *Sharpe's Challenge*, despite coming close, really close, a dozen times, he hasn't been able to get another project off the ground. He has, he says 'a number films in the latter stages of financing'. Muir and Malcolm worked tirelessly to get a new *Sharpe* going, and as often as it was in the 'latter stages of financing', it took years before we all got on the plane to India.

Stuart's older brother was the production supervisor on *Sharpe's Challenge* in India; he works as location manager on other programmes and films. Muir's large-hearted wife, Mercedes has made sure that the brothers are very close, but they're also very different. 'Alex,' says Stuart, 'is a guy who wants a salary every week. He's the smart one of the two. If I'd had that logic, I wouldn't have gone into the film business. I would have gone into banking like all my other friends. The film business here is very,

very tough. Would I like to go to America? At least there, there is a frame-work: distribution, studios, *relationships.*' (The italics are mine.) So why isn't he there now? Because Muir's Spanish partner once told Stuart: 'You go to the States when you're a champ. Not when you're a contender.'

I'm beginning to wonder how you know the difference, or if there is even a difference. Rowan Atkinson in *Johnny English*? A huge hit in the US. Rowan Atkinson in *Keeping Mum*? No US distributor as I write this. Does that make him a champ or a contender? Does every outing start out again as zero sum?

In his publicity shots, Stephen Garrett, a champ for the new television age, looks like a man made for Brut or Cadbury's Roses – sensitive, sexy, lots of shiny hair, soft black jacket over orange t-shirt. He's half of the indie Kudos, creator of *Spooks*, a hit for the BBC. More to the point, *Spooks* is one of the rare British series to play on an American network, albeit arty A&E and renamed *MI-5* (let's not go there). So right now, Garrett's a big noise in the RTS scale of things, but what if the next Kudos' series, *Hustle*, doesn't hustle? Will that send him back to contender status?

Garrett's very clear about what counts as success: 'The holy grail for any producer of TV drama in the UK is the returning series that does that rare thing and actually returns.' So far, *Sharpe* fits the bill. 'If on top of that,' he continues, 'it does that even rarer thing and sells overseas, the "holy grail" gets its inverted commas. A sale to the US is rarer still. When a series is picked up by an American broadcaster the "Holy Grail" goes upper case'. *Sharpe's Challenge* then gets inverted commas, upper case, and success assured. Or does it?

I've said more than once that it doesn't work until it's up on the screen – correction, until it's up on enough screens, preferably 7 million or more television sets, and the right 7 million at that. As Charles Allen said shortly after taking over as chief executive of ITV last year: 'I get £80 a thousand for ABC1s and £8 a thousand for Des.' So heaven help *Sharpe's Challenge* if it doesn't attract enough rugby-loving males and BMW-hankering women. But at least it's going out in America – but even that can't be taken for granted until it's over.

The original *Sharpe* films were picked up by WGBH, the public broadcasting station in Boston. It pulled the series after five episodes, probably, if Garrett is right, because the elements which generated its success in Britain, mitigated against it in the American marketplace. According to Garrett, for 'relevant' read 'parochial' and for 'great British character actors' read 'ugly'. I won't go on but this is why, even after the gentle and experienced *Sharpe's Challenge* editor, Chris Ridsdale, has an almost merciless first cut which is well-paced, exciting, looks gorgeous and has made ITV's Nick Elliott a happy man – Malcolm Craddock is back at the osteopath.

Sean and Toby Stephens: unusual camaraderie on set

The Backroom Boys

It's odd being back on the streets in London. There are missing characters to the story, they were off-stage in India so I set out to find them. The composers, Dominic Muldowney and John Tams, are determined not to be hunted down. Since they have the whole *Sharpe's Challenge* score to write with an 'Indian tone' in less than three weeks, I leave them alone. Others make themselves more accessible which is why I'm here drowning in coffee early this morning, dazed to find myself again with notebook in hand.

Cafés in Soho are mostly grubby affairs. Bits of tuna turning brown, mushy dishes of egg salad and haggard slices of ham waiting for white bread and tasteless cups of tea. Linda's on Poland Street is another sort altogether. No smoking, for a start, and on the walls a dire warning about the horrors of passive smoke and an array of immaculate and up-to-date theatre posters. There are hail-fellow regulars with blunt, expensive haircuts and at a table by the window a typical Linda's conversation which goes thus:

'On the budget we've got, we can't possibly afford names like Kristin Scott-Thomas. Great, but at the end of the day, it'll never happen.'

and:

'Someone like Jeff Goldblum gets good money. You'd have to pay 150,000 up.'

and:

'We'll try but where it's difficult, are you able to make pay-or-play offers?'

and:

'I can ring up CAA in Los Angeles and say "look, there's this small independent film ready to go with funding in place."'

And that's pretty much the end of the meeting for two eager indie producers. The 'we' is a courtesy. Dan Hubbard, casting agent, is being gentle; he knows that funding is almost never in place. Nor will it ever be. And it isn't really 'we' until it is. Besides, as Dan's father John says: 'It happens 20 times a day. We see all these people with absolutely no idea how the business works. They come in saying I wrote this specially for Daniel Day-Lewis or Tom Cruise and they'd be lucky to end up with Ross Kemp.'

Hubbard Casting is the largest of its kind in Britain, probably in Europe. John Hubbard cast all 14 of the early *Sharpe* films, and last summer, *Sharpe's Challenge*. From the start it was clear: no Bean, no Sharpe. Hubbard spent hours as mediating priest, going almost to the wire while he worked out how to get Malcolm Craddock to up the ante sufficiently to satisfy Sean's protective agent. He spent even more hours with lesser and greater agents trying to nail impossible offers on behalf of respected supporting actors whose fees were being whittled down. As soon as the name Toby Stephens came up as first choice for arch-villain Dodd, John said: 'You'll never get him'. Nevertheless, he made it happen. He spent eight sweat-drenched days in Mumbai seeing 200 Indian actors, and at the eleventh hour came up with new ways for Malcolm to oil Sean's faltering deal with Jane Brand at ICM. With agents, it's rarely about loyalty; it's always about 'the deal'. And meanwhile, John was face-to-face casting for a TV series as well as another complicated film.

There can't be an aspiring actor, actress or independent producer in London who doesn't long to be buzzed up to the Hubbards' scruffy two-roomed office above Linda's deli. A surprise would be in store. This is a long, long way from red-carpet glitz: there's a three-bar old-fashioned electric fire, crumbs and stains on cheap blue carpet and DIY shelves which someone must once have meant to paint and fix to the walls.

This is what's meant by film as family: John and Ros Hubbard have been married for 37 years and they run the agency with their 30-year-old son Dan, and 32-year-old daughter Amy who helped to cast *Lord of the Rings* before her baby was born. Amy now works mostly from home, running the firm's business affairs. Of their three assistants: Tom was sent along by Amy's husband, John is the son of Ros's old friend from Dublin, and Kelly was recommended by a powerful agent at PFD. Waste of time, really, combing the media section ads given that 81 per cent of everyone in the British film business is still recruited by word of mouth.

In the tough, bottom-line world of film production today, the term 'casting' is almost a misnomer. It's a Catch 22 world. No point looking for financing until there are big enough names attached to a project to put fire into distribution. No point looking for names until there's funding in place. It's said that 70,000 scripts a year are registered in America alone – last year the American industry made 450 films a year; the British made 37. No wonder that in Hubbard's view: 'nothing moves in the business without a name – even the BBC is name-driven now.'

By his desk, there's an oversized cardboard box overflowing with would-be names, with actors' head-shots and CVs. Hundreds of frozen and enticing glossies, and these are only the unsolicited appeals of the last three months. Maybe someone will get round to seeing five of them; of those, maybe there'll be a part for one. A guest shot, perhaps, in *The Bill*, a call for *Rosemary & Thyme*, rarely a meaty, flamboyant part such as the one in which John Thaw's Inspector Morse was faced down in *Absolute Conviction* by a snake-like embezzler – the young Sean Bean, the year before he went into *Sharpe*. Scenes move too quickly these days. In the new, fast inter-cutting ensemble dramas, dialogue is minimal, three sentences almost a monologue. Sign-posting is all, stereotyping is everything.

Even so, the ever-hopeful John Hubbard still talks about finding *good* actors, *interesting* actors, preferably ones with day jobs. 'Actors' wages are plummeting – everyone under-budgets for talent nowadays. The business has always been cost sensitive but now it's quadrupling cost-sensitive. For the first time in my career, I said to a producer last year: "I'm sorry but I can't work with that money for the actors." I've complained before, but I've never said that. In my experience it's actors and technicians who make the sacrifices. Their money is how they survive, how they pay the mortgage. Financiers' money is never their own. Film money is nobody's money.'

The Hubbard casting fee is £3,500 a week but a project can run intermittently over two years while it stumbles and recovers, and yield as little as £2,000, perhaps £5,000, rarely the £20,000 such a job costs in theory. Yet even now when he describes himself as 'ancient', and the business as 'a complete mess in which there are no rules', John Hubbard still gets seduced into nurturing freebies which climb under his toughened skin. At any one time, he'll have three or four such projects which anyone else would regard as hopeless: a brilliant young Iranian's look at the CIA's illicit backing for the Shah of Iran, another which is a heartbreaker about a priest. He can't help himself, even while the memory stings of helping to put together other such projects, only to hear that another, probably cheaper, casting director was used once the financing fell into place. 'No one appreciates free work,' he says ruefully.

That money becomes the only measure of worth explains, in his view, why so many good scripts aren't made. 'Basically, the film business is now 99.9 per cent about business and even people you admire are dumbing down because their universal masters demand it.' The masters of the film universe are the money.

As the value-chain has changed, so the odds have changed. Simon Shaps, director of television ITV Network, likes to remember that his actor father's fondest wish was 'for me to join the BBC, which represented to him security, a pension and a decent salary. If he said it once, he said it a thousand times.' Not any longer. The BBC is making another savage round of cuts and what Shaps senior would probably be pushing for now is a stint on a reality show, preferably in a rain forest, which appeals to 16–34 year olds with a penchant for foreign cars. According to Dawn Airey, managing director of the Sky networks, 'today reality programmes are the new drama', which doesn't leave many free scheduling hours or budgets for what people such as Malcolm, Muir and John still regard as the real thing.

What Airey calls the 'democratization of television', Hubbard and others unashamedly call 'dumbing down'. Fragmentation of a market faced with not 4 or 5 channels but 400 means that competition sets everyone at each other's throats. The big players, lacking both institutional and personal security, won't or can't work in concert to protect the small, valuable product, let alone its creative source. Or, as Airey puts it: 'Defenders of high culture are never squeamish about vulgar commercialism when there is a deal to be done.'

Small independent producers who use quaint words like 'purity', 'important' and 'integrity' compete for resources in an increasingly unwelcoming market. The best of them live more modestly than they might like to pretend, while the 'big talents' in television make money of an altogether different order. Arguing about 'public service versus populism' over stripped-pine tables in basement kitchens morphs into glittering 'leadership seminars' at the Aspen Institute in the Rockies. Being seen in the VIP section at Live8 passes for philanthropy to those who once shopped at Oxfam and gave to Romanian orphans.

The truth is that for the lucky few, there are sheds-full of money being made in television, and being in on a successful film or a branded format for a new series means that someone somewhere may wake up one day seriously rich. It's seductive. In the way that owning one leg of a racehorse used to be a mark of success among the newly rich, so now is investing in film to the boys from the City. And none of this is a natural habitat for veterans like Hubbard. 'A lot of people are in it for a quick buck. These City guys are brilliant with money but have no idea about film. You sometimes say to them, "Would you like to read the script?" and they say "No". My case rests.'

Hubbard, like Malcolm Craddock and Muir Sutherland, comes from another generation. He's happy to settle for making a comfortable living; his pension is what he calls 'an accident' – he and Ros got into the property market in Ireland when it was one of the poorest, most rundown countries in Europe. So he's in casting as much for creative stimulation as the money, which, at the time we're talking, looks likely to run out in two months. Fortunately, two important series, *Rebus* and *Taggart*, are about to come in, which will more than pay the bills. But his old-fashioned, twentieth-century conditioning has made Hubbard, as he puts it, 'fussy about words'. He picks up a script at random: 'Look at this, it's brilliant. It'll never get made.'

Here's another of those men I've run into time and again: the bright dreamer and avaricious reader who 'failed' at school or, rather, was failed by the school. He's made his own way and the management-speak of twenty-first-century television passes him by. He's buoyed instead by his love of the printed page and the sense that words are important, which has never left him. 'To me it's all about the script. The script is everything.'

Malcolm Craddock wouldn't have commissioned Russell Lewis to write *Sharpe's Challenge* had he not sought a wilier, more penetrating subtext beneath the British militaristic Jingoism and flag-waving. Russell, self-confessed sociopath and 'a bit of an old leftie', says any decent scriptwriter

wears what he calls two hats: 'The PT Barnum hat and your own personal soapbox hat. Yes, we're all aware that in the end it's just a piece of television, but nothing's just a piece of nothing any more. Putting it together in the shadow of Iraq, I didn't want it to be just swords and battles, I didn't want to do Sharpe as froth – I wanted it to have bottom, to put the grit in life's Vaseline. So I thought: "Let's look at the East India Company, let's look at Halliburton."' Not that he counts on his message surviving the final cut. Not every Trojan Horse makes it into Troy.

Still, that being his own gleeful and personal take, he went to the pub with Cornwell's Indian tales and came to terms with the fact that what he was taking on was 'phenomenally difficult'. Going for a beer with a Cornwell book for company was nothing new. 'One of my guilty pleasures has always been to bunk off down to the pub for a packet of dry roast and one of Bernard's. He's fantastic. I love his stuff. He just drives along. To be in the company of such a mind – brilliant. He's the man for me.' Not that he's ever met Bernard. Not that he's ever met Sean Bean either. He saw the actor at the read-through in October. 'It was the first time I'd seen Sean in the flesh and I didn't even say "hello". I'm desperately shy, particularly of new people in a huge gathering, which is why I do what I do – it keeps me in a room by myself.'

We meet for coffee at La Strada outside the Festival Hall on the South Bank. In order to smoke, we persuade the reluctant waiter to serve us outside. I'm wearing a thick anorak, hat, scarf, gloves, boots – and freeze. It takes hours to notice that Russell in a jacket and shirt has turned blue. His own fault. He's far too good company. Sure enough, here's another bright, idiosyncratic drop-out, this time of the stage school his parents pushed him into. 'I was a TV kid, that's my education but I always read from a young age, a very young age. I'd read anything and everything. Books – I found them great company.'

There was a decade of messing about after leaving school at 16 – getting by in a band for a few years, temping as an Office Angel, stacking a warehouse out by the airport and some typecasting as Debenham's Santa Claus which he describes as 'horrible'. Typecasting because at first it's hard to see Russell inside all those whiskers: a grisard of a beard, a bush of hair barely held in check by a pony-tail, tiny gold-rimmed varifocals and the hunched shoulders of a writer who can work, if needed, 48 or even 72 hours straight 'on willpower and coffee'.

Challenge wasn't his first *Sharpe* script. He wrote *Sharpe's Battle* for the third series in which Wellington sticks the now Major Sharpe with the Spanish king's gift of his useless ceremonial guard, the Royal Irish Company. Watch that episode carefully and hidden in the butchering and betrayal, courage and nail-biting survival, is a comment about the occupation of Ireland by the English, of the ironic fact that over a third of Wellington's army was Irish, while, half a century after the massacre at Culloden, many were Scottish. In Lewis's take on *Sharpe*, loyalty is a tangled spider's web, and where there is no law, morality is vested in the search for personal justice with or without honour. 'It's little things, really, little signposts which point the way to where the author's head and heart are at.'

When he wrote *Battle* in 1995, he was still being described as one of television's 'rising stars'. Now he's in his 40s, at the top, and can choose what he writes. Why *Challenge*? 'I adore *Sharpe*, that's the main reason I did it. It's a lovely gig.' First came his favourite part – 'shed-loads of digging' on both the history and the nightmarish geography of India, since whatever he promised Malcolm Craddock, he never had the slightest intention of going out there to see for himself. There were characters to invent and others to drop, finding ways to knit together complicated story lines into 140 minutes of screen time. 'It was a mad, mad brief.'

Originally there were twin sisters for Sharpe to rescue – 'one feisty, one a milksop'. One sister had to go: the milksop. Given the traditional *Sharpe* take on women, I hadn't recognized Celia as the feisty one. In India, I winced when Madhuvanthi, the evil power-hungry concubine, who could give Disney's queen in *Snow White* a good run, had the Indian princess flogged. 'It is particularly nasty, I suppose, and not a particular peccadillo of mine, but we lost the tiger and perhaps it was something to put Madhuvanthi beyond the pale. She's not a pantomime figure but not far off it. No hiding place I'm afraid'. Another thoughtful drag on a Silk Cut, and then the come-back: 'We've flogged Sharpe in the past, you know, how about equality and all that?'

I can imagine Malcolm Craddock agonizing over every word of Russell's drafts. The producer runs *Sharpe* like a military machine, or rather the compassionate, honourable military machine we'd like to believe in, thinking of Deep Cut – and, yes, that comes up in conversation with Russell. It's a relief, after the film-set hothouse, to be able to really talk again and he roams wide and pinkish. He scours buses, pubs and newspapers for people, dialogue, stories, the way language changes and concerns arise and disappear.

It's a shame he's never met Sean. They share a shyness mitigated by the speed of a lizard's tongue when challenged, and a wily ability to listen. I ask how hard it is to write Sean's voice and delivery without ever having spent time with him. 'I think it's a bit akin to mimicry. It's over-empathising – it's what sociopaths do when they're with someone they've not met before. They mirror the person they're with. I couldn't tell you how but I know how Richard Sharpe sounds in my head.'

What drives him mad is when people say they're 'working for film' and they're not. They're working for television. 'TV is what it is – it's not film because you don't have anything like the resources. That's good because it's a lot wordier, there's more dialogue. I love language and without the tools to express yourself, it has to affect the way you think. Inarticulacy has to make you cross. There's a real poverty of language now and it leaves me sad.'

Asked which of his scripts he would be proudest of, he mentions *Without Motive*, which prompts this very revealing outpouring. 'It tried to depict a very long murder investigation and the effect of failure upon decent policemen. The bigger picture was that it was a piece about men and women – what level of violence against women is seemingly acceptable in society. How that viewpoint changes when the victim is suddenly no longer a prostitute but an "innocent" young student. I remember looking at one particular copy of the *Daily Mirror* of all things – on one page was the usual rabid frothing about paedophiles and sex offenders in our midst, while on the opposite page was a photograph of Charlotte Church's backside – she would have been just about 16 – as she had "won" Rear of the Year. I kept the pieces pinned to the wall to look at whenever I felt in danger of losing my anger. I think it was Joe Orton who wrote: "Cleanse my heart, give me the ability to rage correctly."'

So even when he describes *Sharpe's Challenge* as 'an entertaining ride', he also reminds me that the great Dennis Potter said 'fight, kick and bite to get on television. That's where the audience is; that's where the nation's heart rests.'

When Malcolm and Muir met ITV's controller of drama, Nick Elliott, for a friendly lunch at Elena's L'Etoile on Charlotte Street in August 2004, *Sharpe's Challenge* wasn't anywhere near a script. As a project, it didn't exist. The producers had invested two years trying to put together a feature film, *Sharpe's Tiger*, based on Bernard's original Indian novels. It involved Sharpe as a 25-year-old all the way through, unfortunate as that sounds – a grizzly tiger, and a really expensive film script which never quite worked.

Like so many projects, it cost money – £90,000 in all – to develop and recce, nearly happened, and never made it. There had been hopes of a Canadian co-production involving a complicated tax-credit deal for investors, which could have been spread over the cost of shooting in India as a co-Commonwealth country, owing to an even more complicated set of tax laws. It all looked cheerfully hopeful for a while. Another blind alley.

To some extent, the timing of the lunch with Nick Elliott was lucky. Terrestrial TV wasn't, and isn't, having a very good decade. Even ignoring the way ITV was about to fall apart at the top, it's a question of changing demographics and viewing habits and what they do to the cash flow. Commercial television was born to a Britain which had benefited from the 1944 Education Act and still took its culture seriously. It paid attention to television, even (or especially) when it was pushing such novelties as washing powder and processed food. Trust Melvyn Bragg to get it right: 'In 1955, two out of five Brits did not clean their teeth. ITV changed all that with a new ad which was for Gibbs toothpaste.'

As recently as 10 years ago, an audience of 10 million with a 40 per cent share was fairly normal for ITV. Today, a 6 million rating with a 26% share might count as a respectable hit, and too often ITV's core audience is made up of or, more importantly, *perceived* as made up of Northern working-class pensioners. Not too much incentive there for advertisers of upmarket financial services, long-haul airlines and nippy foreign cars. And if the cash isn't going to come from the ads, who's going to pay for the programmes which punctuate them?

Welcome to the iPod era. People who've got the hang of making their own music mixes won't take long to start picking and choosing their own television schedules. Hence the belief that there's power in a successful series which commands if not loyalty, at least familiarity. Take a random week and of the top 20 network programmes, 15 will probably be episodes of soaps and the other 5 regular, weekly series such as *Heartbeat*. Maybe a *Match of the Day* will make it into the top 25. It's why ITV spends money on Formula 1 and football: very ABC1 males. It explains *Footballers' Wives*: very female, very London, very 16–34, very Renault Clio.

It's why there is talk of bringing back *Rumpole of the Bailey*, even without the deceased Leo McKern, and Sergeant Lewis came back, without his boss, John Thaw as Inspector Morse. *Rumpole* and *Morse*, like *Sharpe*, are brands. What's even more appealing about brand *Sharpe* is that Sean Bean is alive and a bigger star than ever (a plus, yes, but a minus in terms of, right again, money). To boot, *Sharpe* in its day was unusual in delivering an audience almost evenly divided between women and those elusive ABC males, and despite 8 years' absence, still has a feverish following. There were half a million hits on the *Sharpe* appreciation society's website last year, just one of many devoted to Bean-counting.

Still, no doubt about it, when Malcolm and Muir casually brought up *Sharpe* over the white linen tablecloths at Elena's L'Etoile, Nick and his then number two, Jenny, might have seemed mad to tell them to follow it up officially with A Meeting. Compared to the cheaper and malicious pleasure to be had watching celebrities munching on insects in the jungle and being buried in rats, not many controllers of drama would have jumped at the idea of an old-fashioned, period drama about the Raj to be shot in India. Not exactly Dickens, hardly Jane Austen, definitely not Paul Abbot's *Shameless* (the latest harrowing 'big thing'), not very BAFTA for sure.

Well, *Sharpe* didn't win BAFTAs even at its height, and gambling on an 8 million plus audience for the Imperial Brits mightn't seem an inviting bet to any mindful Oxford graduate of modern history, let alone one who's a rare survivor of 40 years in telly. Nick Elliott probably has the largest budget at the ITV network centre. However much Muir resents my saying this, Nick is an odd sight in the ITV headquarters in the Gray's Inn Road. Picture this: floor upon floor of little glass boxes around a tall, inward-looking atrium, hundreds of 20/30-somethings in front of computer screens and tucked into a corner on the fifth floor, this white, silky-haired, soft-skinned, lovely 60-something in expensive pink shirt bulging over years of good food and drink.

This glass palace exists to spend a billion pounds a year, of which, very roughly, £300 to £350 million is ear-marked for drama. Most of that is for returning shows – primarily soap operas, but also such innocuous fare as white, middle-England's *Midsomer Murders* and a few, increasingly fewer, special events. Special events are what you splash around the Sunday papers, or at least the *Radio Times*: *Sharpe's Challenge*, for instance.

Now if there's one thing guaranteed to nettle the smooth and charming Elliott, it's talk of the Golden Age of the 1960s, and the dumbing down of the present. It's as if all those earnest and soul-searching articles on the issue in the Royal Television Society's thoughtful magazine for the industry's top people never existed.

The golden age? The passionate, politically and socially resonant drama of the sixties? 'Another piece of myth from the chattering classes,' he scoffs. 'Folklore for *Guardian* readers. Utter bollocks. People feel better about being snobbish about TV. They prefer a self-image that puts about that they read novels, go to French films and never watch *Big Brother*. My memory is cynical about the past because I was there. TV in the past was absolute crap. It was wall to wall Hughie Green's *Opportunity Knocks*. Drama? Mean, gritty little left-wing shits who spit and hate the world don't make heroes.'

I'm reminded of something said earlier this year, if with a tad more humour, by Andy Allen (the original backer of *Sharpe*): 'I tire easily of the talk about the golden age of ITV. The "we were the lucky ones" seems to have very little to do with programmes and an awful lot to do with lunch. In the 1960s, if somebody entered an office and said, "I've had an idea", chances were his next words would be, "Let's go to the Caprice, I'm so bored with the Mirabelle".

Now to be fair to Nick Elliott, surely a captivating man when he doesn't feel that he's being got at in this darkened palace of dreams, there's more to ITV's credit than *Coronation Street* and *The Bill*. He once headed up the BBC's drama as well as London Weekend Television's and any talk of the past ought to mention more recent landmarks such as Robbie Coltrane and *Cracker*, Helen Mirren and *Prime Suspect*, the Hillsborough disaster, *Bloody Sunday*, Ray Winstone, Julie Walters and Brenda Blethyn in major vehicles. Let's remember that the much-admired HBO network in America puts out awful rubbish as well as *The Sopranos* and *Six Feet Under*.

But *Sharpe's Challenge* isn't rubbish, it's expensive and it's period, which is unfashionable at the moment unless it can be made 'contemporary' (Joe Wright's *Pride & Prejudice*) or, nudge nudge, can deliver loudly enough a moral for society today (BBC's *Bleak House*). More barely concealed impatience from Nick Elliott.

'I want to be interested in character and stories I haven't heard a million times. *Sharpe* was a big, very successful title in ITV's history with exciting, much-loved stories. It has colour, action, escapism and yes, there was a British Empire and there were British soldiers and, frankly, when it came up I didn't worry about political sensitivities. And Sean Bean's the most handsome beast, sexy, athletic and a hero.'

But then he says something which hangs over me afterwards. 'The purpose of all written fiction is to tell a story. It doesn't have to tell you anything else. Shakespeare wrote *A Midsummer Night's Dream*. What was that? It was a story about people.'

Forget cannon and explosives, forget stuntmen plunging from battlements, *Sharpe's Challenge* is a story about people. It's about the desperate conflict between two men who found in each other both resemblance and

difference. Because of Toby's strength, he was able to mirror what the embittered Sharpe might have become, might still become. It's about the way power uses the weak, in this case the young Maharajah, but how luck, call it fate, can vouchsafe someone a second chance, as it has Sharpe. It's about the devotion that friendship can inspire – the care and love in Harper's face when Sharpe is tried to the edge of his being. There were moments on set when I felt drawn inside the characters' very skin, so forceful was the emotional rhythm of the actors.

When I wrote in India, it was with a storm of Pink Floyd on my laptop or headphones. This isn't a personal red herring, by the way. It helps me to understand what Chris Ridsdale, the *Sharpe's Challenge* editor is talking about when I go to the cutting room. The many layers of the Floyd's music drives it forward and yet, even after weeks, I find new ones. The emotional pace can switch in an instant and I'm always waiting for, and never tire of, the heart-breaking cry of David Gilmour's guitar. I can't say that my neighbours at the Samode Palace Hotel shared my enthusiasm, in fact according to the front desk, they didn't.

So, equally, I have to wonder how much of what moved me on set in

India will be shared by others once it's cut and on the screen. And how much will even get there, and work when it does. Chris Ridsdale is, well, you'll have guessed by now, another school 'failure'. His quantity surveyor father was 'in despair'. He floundered around until his family doctor talked to a patient who was a producer who got him a job as a second assistant editor. 'That was it really.'

He's in his attractive 50s with cropped grey hair, smart Soho black and extremely sore eyes. For all his charm, he's an impatient man. I suspect impatience is the one quality a good editor needs. If TV ever was a patient medium, it isn't now. On the old *Sharpe*s, you could count on a minute of screen time per script page; on *Sharpe's Challenge* it's down to 30 seconds. And to know how slow that action still is for today's generation, watch music videos.

Chris cuts for pace and rhythm; they're what set the emotional line of a scene, allow the time to linger, or dictate those other times when the beat's too short to hold a moment however strong the acting. What he calls 'disciplined', I'd call ruthless. He's paring away anything which holds up the story, while not gutting its emotional intensity. At the same time he's seeking layers of meaning communicated in the shortest time. Take the stirring sword fight between Dodd and Sharpe in the parade ground. 'I've never cut a sword fight in my life and I'm making up for that with a vengeance.' All those hours in the sun? Running now at 1 minute 51 seconds. There's a brief cut-away to Celia and Madhuvanthi: one instant is all there is in which to suggest the two women's growing interest in Sharpe. Too long, and the viewer will grind her teeth wanting to get back to Sean and Toby. Too short, and a whole series of signals will be missed. I understand director Alan Pakula's cry for an editor with 'magic fingers'.

It's a somewhat voyeuristic occupation. Tom Clegg was right there – the action happened to and around him. Chris is going backwards and forwards on a computer looking at the story from a distance while trying at the same time to operate within it. Doesn't he miss the artistry of cutting real tape, the thrill of the razor? He snorts. 'This is just a machine, a tool. There's no artistry in taking an hour to do what I can do in five minutes.' He's ruled by time: five acts of 14 minutes minimum for four ad breaks,

15–20 seconds to be left for the second instalment teaser, two weeks until it's shown to ITV, four weeks until it's locked off for dubbing, the time of his Friday night train home to Devon.

But this isn't *his* film. The first cut (he hates the word 'rough') was his in a way but always Tom Clegg's. The rushes came back with script supervisor Caroline O'Reilly's meticulous notes and marked-up script. Tom made it known what he wanted on the screen. He still does. He works at Chris's shoulder. 'He's a lovely man,' the editor says with feeling. 'He knows exactly what he wants, doesn't pick at things for the sake of picking at things. Tom hasn't got an ego – he's not that kind of man. If I was under the kind of pressure he was making this film … well, I can't imagine it.'

While I'm watching the staggering explosion of Jaigarh's mined tunnel (Nigel and the boys of SFX take a bow), in walks Tom in elegant linen shirt and sleek black corduroys. I find again the relaxed and mischievous man I met in Jaipur months ago. I see it in his eyes, the looseness of his body. When I hear later that Nick Elliott was delighted when he saw *Sharpe's Challenge*, I was surprised to be pleased for the director. Like Sharpe, in a complicated world and against the odds, Tom Clegg got his character back.

Out-Takes

Re-entry from India is a mystery. Gareth Milne is taken to hospital – I get e-mails from Tony Auger of Special Effects asking for news of the stunt co-ordinator who, in turn, asks for news of Tony. Nigel Willoughby meets me in Bertorelli's at lunchtime and we leave as the supper crowd arrive. E-mails come in asking how he's doing – e-mails to me. Clearly, by keeping in touch, I'm committing a film world faux pas. 'On location doesn't count', the industry's slogan, isn't only about affairs; it seems to be about friendships too.

Pride probably has something to do with it. Of the 25,000 or so people working in British film and television production, over 70 per cent are unemployed at some point in the year, and half of these for three months or more. This is a particularly bleak January. Perhaps this is more tough-guy/boys' stuff: not wanting to admit to being hard up, not wanting to seem to be scrounging for jobs.

On the other hand, a chatty e-mail arrives from Emma Pike, production manager, off in Thailand, trying to decide whether the industry is worth it, or whether the upholstery course she took last year should be the next act. Why do women stick it out? They not only earn less than men but almost certainly won't be either married or part of a couple, compared with 69 per cent of their male colleagues who are.

I'm particularly touched when Julia Stannard, the tough, bright, good-looking co-producer tells me quite matter-of-factly, 'You have to give up any idea of being popular in this job. But I'll settle for the fact that if there's dislike, it's at least coupled with respect'. Julia never takes time off if she can help it. She did no less than 20 different budgets for *Sharpe's Challenge*, while working on Nicholas Hytner's *History Boys*. She finished on that film the day she left for India. In Julia's life plan, if you want to be a producer, sacrifice is what it takes.

I watch the old *Sharpes* and find myself held to ransom again by the futile death of David Ashton's Major Lennox, by competing notions of honour and the ethical problem of sacrificing men for political ends. Each episode leaves me grappling to understand, through Sharpe's inner battles, terms which are alien to me – patriotism, glory, honour, victory in death. What I'm really gnawing over is whether, in the end, we can only recover and interpret the meanings of social actions from the point of view of the agents performing them. What can be more relevant than that to today's multi-cultural Britain? In Sharpe's so-called old-fashioned storytelling, I'm back at the very heart of the philosophy of social science. Yes, this is indeed where I came in.

One more hook remains to close the circle. On a cold Monday evening, I meet Sean in the pub where I first interviewed him last spring. Given the chance, this intelligent, wily actor will skim along the surface, monosyllabic for choice, anything to keep the stranger at bay. Dig at him, poke and hostility surfaces in broken appointments, a cutting coldness on set and an ability to look straight through you in passing.

The Sean I meet this time is different. He's a man who trusts with reluctance: 'I trust my friends. I trust my family'. How often has he said that in the past. Now, there's a sense of a line crossed. 'I've got to know you. It's a weird situation being interviewed – it isn't real.' *Real*, the word he uses so often – but the artificiality of interviewing or filming, doesn't explain why he often seemed so cold to crew members with whom he was quite happy to get pissed.

'It came as a bit of a shock to play Sharpe again. I think I underestimated the responsibility in front of me. It was scary. It's always scary. You never know, you *never* know, if you're going to succeed. You might be shitting yourself inside but you can't afford to show it and maybe to outsiders it might be misinterpreted as being cold, but, if it does, it doesn't really bother me. You're exploring very deep-seated emotions in the character, but it's a character, it's not me – and I think you have to separate the two. That's what I try to do to keep my sanity, but sometimes it can cross over. At certain times, on certain days it's the same as when you have a nightmare. You wake up the next day, you know it was a bad dream but it's still disturbing. It stays with you.'

Once again, I came up against the way I'd accepted the received wisdom about him as reality. Sean didn't like being in India, it was said; he didn't go anywhere because he isn't interested in anything except beer, football and Sheffield United. Forget India, forget elephants, forget thrills, the film hinges on Sean. And, yes, he felt that pressure and, yes, he wants to go back to Rajasthan. Besides, while he may not bother with actors or crew when the job's done, he talks of Punya, his Rajput assistant, as a friend, of his dignity, honesty, of how *real* he was. 'I felt really sad when I came back. It's taking time to wear off. We're all different but it's important to switch off, to lead a normal life.'

A normal life? What's that to an actor who's so suspicious of people that almost everyone except old, old friends have to communicate with him through his agent? 'Have breakfast, listen to the radio, read the papers, go to the dentist … Fuck me, I don't know what a normal life is …' and then a flash of mischief '… and practise me snogging'.

It's a dig at that talk weeks ago in the quiet Samode night when I said I'd never seen him do genuine intimacy on screen with a woman. But the Warner Brothers' film, *North Country*, has just come out and in it he plays scenes with Frances McDormand of such tenderness and warmth that he's unrecognizable from the early Sean Bean.

Many – maybe most – actors get stuck in their first success, become a parody of their boyish selves as they get older. In subtle ways, Sean the actor has deepened and reached beyond his apparent boundaries, as the older Sharpe did in India. So, despite his successes in Hollywood, maybe Richard Sharpe is still Sean's personal touchstone. 'A lot of times Sharpe had to state his position when he was right up against it. He was a loner and he remained a loner up to the end. He was a man of courage and strength and he wouldn't take crap from nobody.' Resonances there with Sean, which perhaps explains his ambivalence when he had to get on that plane to India and face 'himself' nine years on. I still wouldn't be surprised that if I should ever run into Sean again, he acts as if we've never met. He's a strange man.

Like Sean, I'm still touched by the intensity of the weeks in Jaipur, Samode and Jodphur, by the way small moments cut like a knife with the realization that they're over. Memories fade and people drift away into ordinariness. There's no going back.

As I write this, there's a phone call from Alistair Crocker in Bristol. 'Let's meet up for lunch', he says, 'and we can talk about India, reminisce about the old days and what a good time we had. A bit of nostalgia'.

At the gym last night, I caught the first 'ad' for *Sharpe*. It's being pushed as one of four 'event' dramas. But when the 'event' has been gobbled up by the small screen, when the hurrahs are over, when even my memories have faded, the beauty of India and the drama of the story will be there always in *Sharpe's Challenge*. For me, that's the real magic of television.

Acknowledgments

First, I want to thank my fearsome and wonderful agent, Toby Eady, who put up with me through book suggestions which could have had at best a readership of two – my children, Eben and Kate, whose loyalty buoyed me during the months in India.

Susan Watt of Harper Collins has been *Sharpe's Tiger* on my behalf and kindness itself to me. Malcolm Craddock and Julia Stannard responded with heroic promptness to my emails seeking clarification and details. Malcolm's trust never wavered (or if it did, he sheltered me from it). He thought he was going to get, and I quote: 'a nice little book as a souvenir for us all to show our grandchildren.' He didn't, but nor did he complain. Muir Sutherland bore me with patience and generosity. Catherine Best proof-read as I went along and her help was invaluable, as it has always been. Clare Hey's smile lit up some difficult corners.

On the night before the last shooting day in Jodphur, I agreed to let Sean Bean read everything I'd written about him. My condition was that no one else should see it. I found out from Punya that he had hidden the pages under the mattress in his trailer overnight. That was the moment I finally warmed to him. His requests for changes were so tiny that my lack of trust in insisting he initial everything was all too clear. But he did so with grace, and I hope he'll forgive me.

The friendship and support of Susan Richards and Anthony Smith instilled courage and rationality, when both failed. And such rationality as

I have is due to my colleagues at Birkbeck College and the experience of teaching questing students on the BA (Hons) degree in Politics, Philosophy and History. I have missed them.

For the crew of *Sharpe's Challenge*, I will always feel gratitude and lasting affection.

LB
Arbroath, March 2005